ADULT ALL-IN-ONE COURSE

LESSON · THEORY · SOLO

FOREWORD

The goal of Level 3 of Alfred's Basic Adult All-in-One Course is to provide, within one book, a flexible and highly enjoyable presentation of lesson, theory and solo material. This will allow the student to progress smoothly and easily, without gaps, toward playing in some of the more advanced keys, as well as playing some of the great masterworks of piano literature.

The book is divided into four sections:

1. A REVIEW OF OLD KEY SIGNATURES (but with some new concepts added).
2. NEW KEY SIGNATURES AND CONCEPTS.
3. "JUST FOR FUN" MUSIC. These pieces are scattered throughout the book and are included for relaxation and amusement. They may be played whenever the student wishes.
4. "AMBITIOUS" SECTION. This section is for the student who is willing to devote a little extra effort toward learning some of the great masterworks that require a bit of additional practice. They are within the capabilities of anyone who has completed the previous books of this series and the first three sections of this book.

The book closes with a *Dictionary of Musical Terms*.

The authors are confident that the selection of material for this book will provide the student with a great variety of pleasing music to play, since it includes many familiar favorites, along with a variety of effective original keyboard compositions.

Willard A. Palmer
Morton Manus
Amanda Vick Lethco

Alfred Music
P.O. Box 10003
Van Nuys, CA 91410-0003
alfred.com

ISBN-10: 0-7390-0068-3 (Book)
ISBN-13: 978-0-7390-0068-7 (Book)

ISBN-10: 0-7390-7534-9 (Book & CD)
ISBN-13: 978-0-7390-7534-0 (Book & CD)

Cover photo: Jeff Oshiro

Contents

SECTION 3
Ambitious Selections

A SUPER-SPECIAL SORTA SONG!

This book begins with a piece that is just for fun. There are more "JUST FOR FUN" pieces in this book on pages 28, 72 and 88. You may play them at any time.

Moderate & relaxed

Play eighth notes in long-short pairs.

Willard A. Palmer

LH staccato

mf Oh, what fun it is to play pi - an - o When ya

sing a spe - cial song that makes ya smile like a Pol - ly - an - na. I could sit and play it

all day long, be - cause it's such a sup - er - spec - ial sort - a song! *f* And the beat is so

Optional 2nd verse: Light and easy, play it bright and breezy,
And this super-special song will make you smile like the "Mona Leezy."
It's all right, it never can be wrong,
Because it's such a super-special sorta song!

And the beat is so neat, *etc.*

1. neat,
2. play,

And the notes are so nice,
And the rhythm's so right,

That I'm tap-pin' my feet,
I could play it all day!

And I'm play-in' it
I could play it all

twice!
night!

It's a pleas-ure to

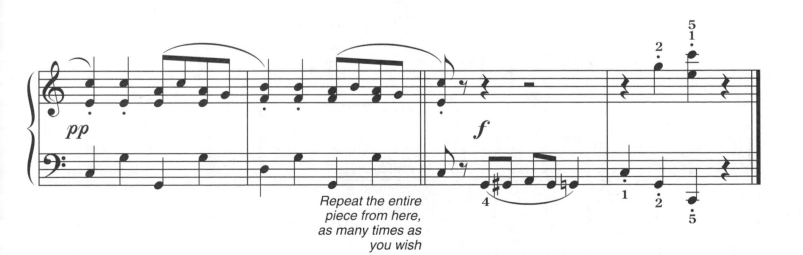

*Repeat the entire
piece from here,
as many times as
you wish*

Calypso Rhumba

A STUDY IN OVERLAPPING PEDALING

KEY OF C MAJOR
Key Signature: no ♯, no ♭.

Andante moderato

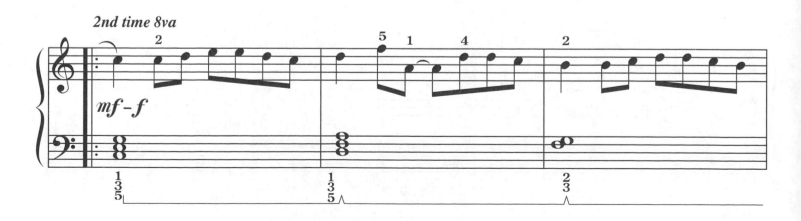

*Play eighth notes evenly!

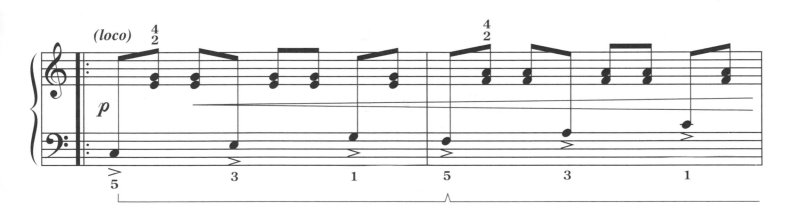

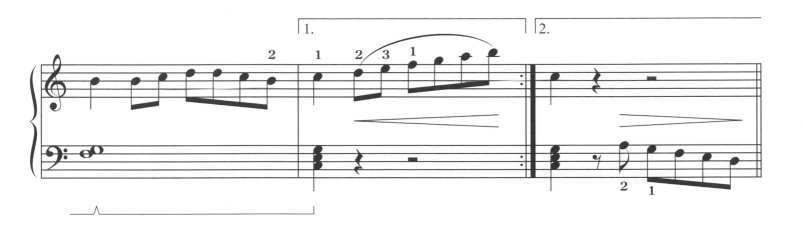

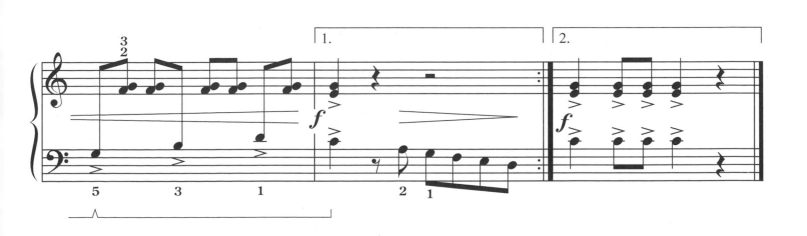

Scale Degrees: Tonic, Dominant, Subdominant

The tones of a scale are also called the *degrees* of the scale. Each *scale degree* has a name.
- The KEY-NOTE (the tone of the same name as the scale) is called the **TONIC.**
- The tone a 5th ABOVE the tonic is called the **DOMINANT.**
- The tone a 5th BELOW the tonic is called the **SUBDOMINANT.**

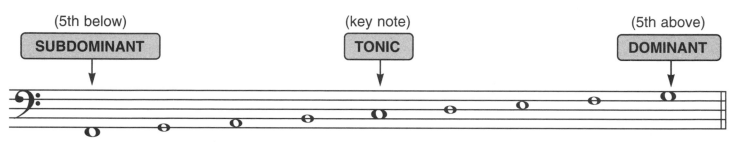

REMEMBER: SUB means "below" or "under." (SUBmarine, SUBway, etc.)

KEY OF C MAJOR

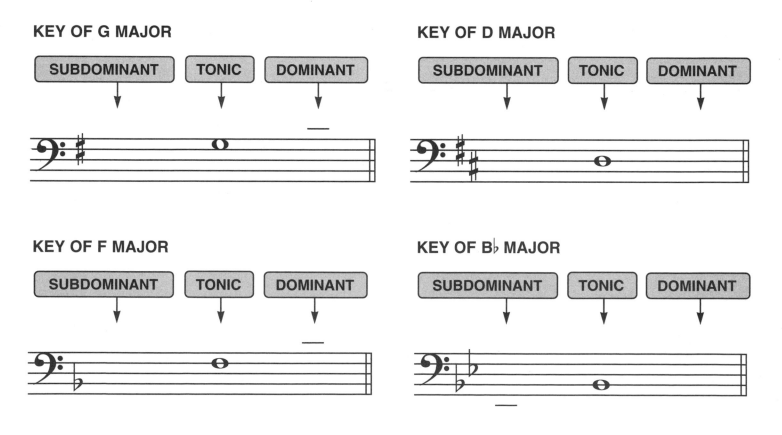

1. Write the SUBDOMINANT and DOMINANT degrees for each TONIC note given below:

KEY OF G MAJOR

KEY OF D MAJOR

KEY OF F MAJOR

KEY OF B♭ MAJOR

2. Write the answers in the blanks:

C is the TONIC in the key of _____ major.   G is the DOMINANT in the key of _____ major.
C is the DOMINANT in the key of _____ major.   C is the SUBDOMINANT in the key of _____ major.

Writing the Dominant

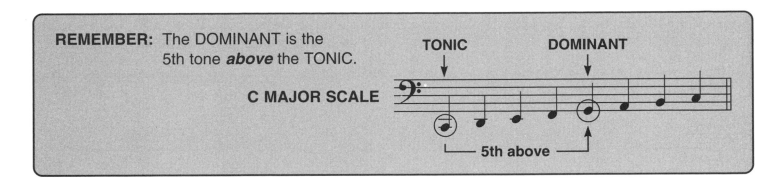

REMEMBER: The DOMINANT is the 5th tone *above* the TONIC.

TONIC   DOMINANT

C MAJOR SCALE

5th above

In the five scales below:

1. Circle all the TONIC notes.
2. Circle all the DOMINANT notes.

C MAJOR SCALE

G MAJOR SCALE

D MAJOR SCALE

F MAJOR SCALE

B♭ MAJOR SCALE

Writing the Subdominant

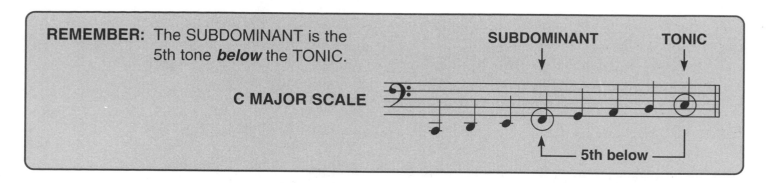

REMEMBER: The SUBDOMINANT is the 5th tone *below* the TONIC.

C MAJOR SCALE

1. Circle all the SUBDOMINANT notes in the five scales on page 9.
2. Play each circled note, saying the name of the scale degree (tonic, subdominant or dominant).

THE SCALE DEGREES ARE NUMBERED WITH ROMAN NUMERALS.

TONIC = I   **DOMINANT = V**   **SUBDOMINANT = IV**

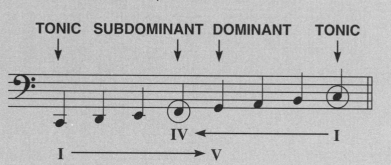

IMPORTANT! The subdominant is numbered **IV** because of its position in the scale. It is NOT called "subdominant" because it is just below the dominant. It is called "subdominant" because it is the same distance BELOW the tonic as the dominant is ABOVE the tonic!

In the four scales below:
1. Write **I** below each TONIC note.
2. Write **V** below each DOMINANT note.
3. Write **IV** below each SUBDOMINANT note.

G MAJOR SCALE

F MAJOR SCALE

D MAJOR SCALE

B♭ MAJOR SCALE

4. On page 9, write **I** below each TONIC note, **V** below each DOMINANT note, and **IV** below each SUBDOMINANT note.

Reviewing: The Circle of 5ths

Using the **Circle of 5ths,** the TONIC, DOMINANT and SUBDOMINANT of any scale may be found quickly and easily.

- Take any letter on the circle as the key note or TONIC.
- The next letter clockwise is the DOMINANT.
- The next letter counter-clockwise is the SUBDOMINANT.

Example: Take C as the tonic. The DOMINANT is G. The SUBDOMINANT is F.

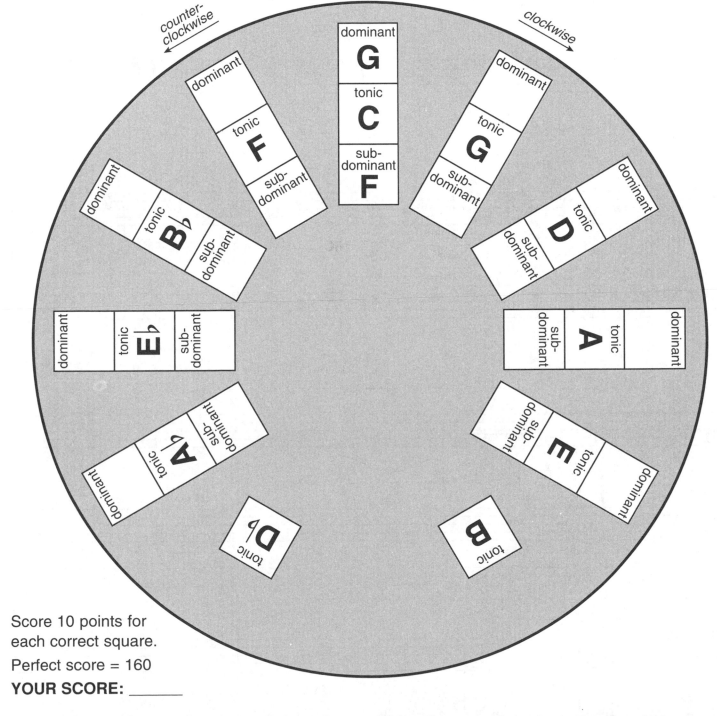

Score 10 points for
each correct square.

Perfect score = 160

YOUR SCORE: _____

1. Write the DOMINANT note for each given TONIC in the square *above* it, turning the circle as you write. The answer will be the same as the next tonic note clockwise.

2. Write the SUBDOMINANT note for each given TONIC in the square *below* it, turning the circle as you write. The answer will be the same as the next tonic note counter-clockwise.

The squares above and below C are filled in as examples.

FANDANGO

The *FANDANGO* is a lively Spanish dance with three beats per measure. It is usually based on this chord progression:

KEY OF A MINOR*
Key Signature: no ♯, no ♭.

Reminder: A MINOR is the *relative minor* of the key of C MAJOR. Both keys have the same key signature.

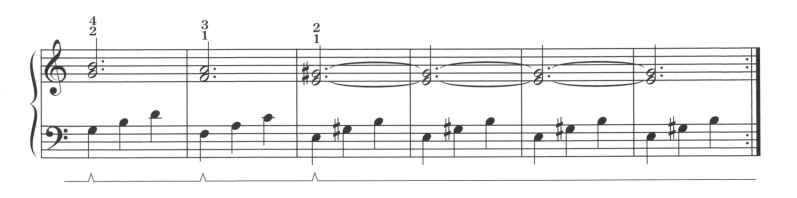

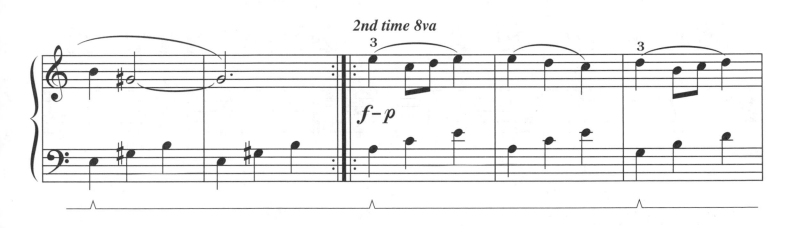

D. C. al Fine

More Scale Degrees: Mediant & Submediant

- The **MEDIANT** is the 3rd degree *above* the TONIC (*midway* between the tonic and dominant).
- The **SUBMEDIANT** is the 3rd *below* the TONIC (*midway* between the tonic and subdominant).

Mediant is a Latin word meaning "in the middle."

KEY OF C MAJOR

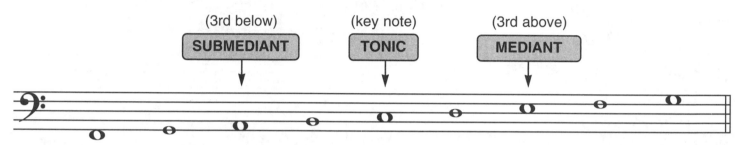

1. Write the SUBMEDIANT and MEDIANT degrees for each TONIC note given below:

KEY OF G MAJOR

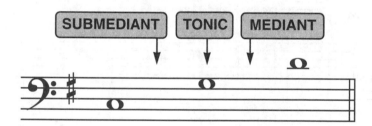

KEY OF D MAJOR

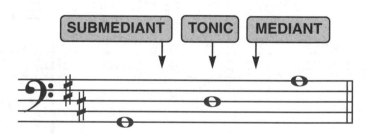

KEY OF F MAJOR

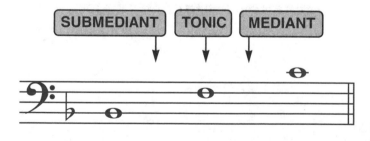

KEY OF B♭ MAJOR

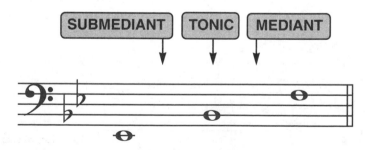

2. Write the answers in the blanks:

A is the MEDIANT in the key of _____ major.

A is the SUBMEDIANT in the key of _____ major.

A is the DOMINANT in the key of _____ major.

A is the TONIC in the key of _____ major.

Writing the Mediant

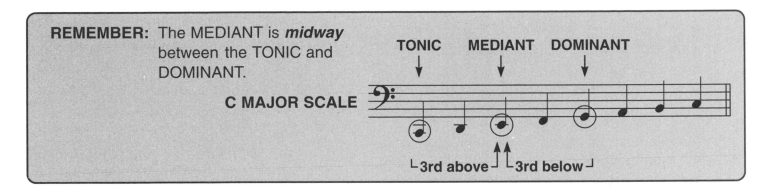

REMEMBER: The MEDIANT is *midway* between the TONIC and DOMINANT.

In the scales below:

1. Circle all the TONIC notes.
2. Circle all the DOMINANT notes.
3. Circle all the MEDIANT notes.

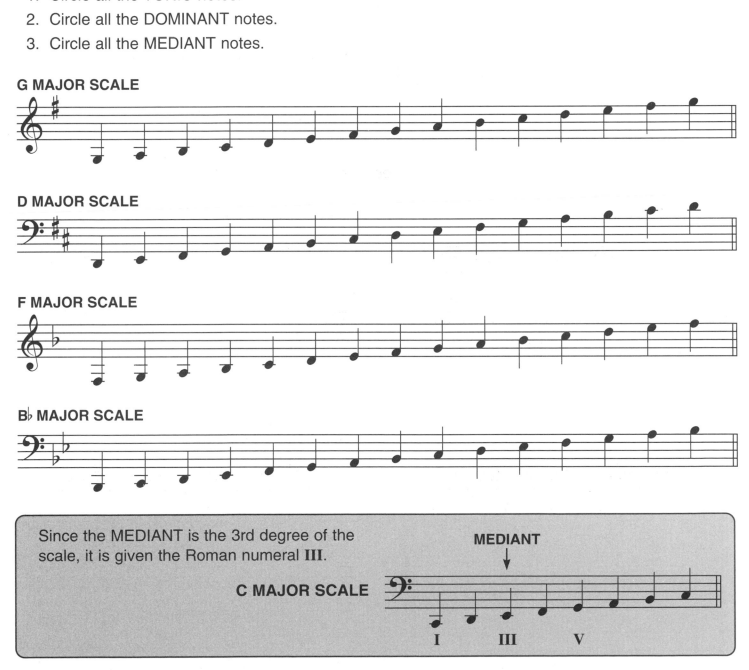

G MAJOR SCALE

D MAJOR SCALE

F MAJOR SCALE

B♭ MAJOR SCALE

Since the MEDIANT is the 3rd degree of the scale, it is given the Roman numeral **III**.

C MAJOR SCALE

4. In the four scales above, write **I** below each TONIC, **III** below each MEDIANT, and **V** below each DOMINANT.

Writing the Submediant

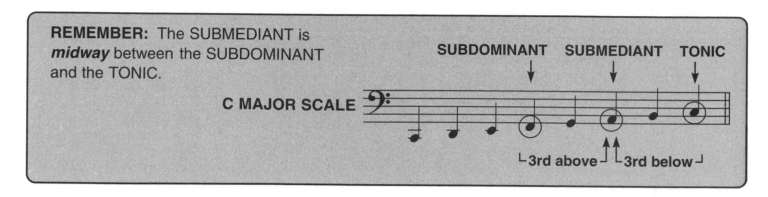

REMEMBER: The SUBMEDIANT is *midway* between the SUBDOMINANT and the TONIC.

In the scales below:

1. Circle all the TONIC notes.
2. Circle all the SUBDOMINANT notes.
3. Circle all the SUBMEDIANT notes.

G MAJOR SCALE

D MAJOR SCALE

F MAJOR SCALE

B♭ MAJOR SCALE

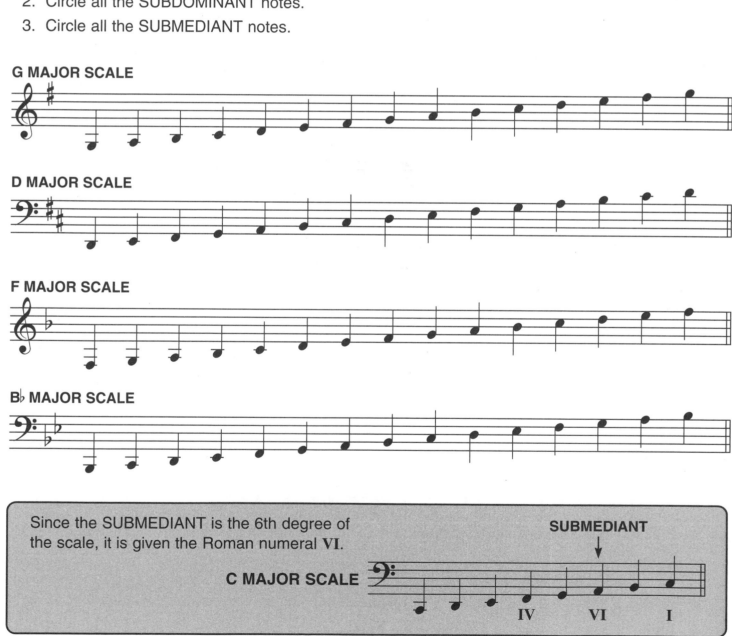

Since the SUBMEDIANT is the 6th degree of the scale, it is given the Roman numeral **VI**.

4. In the four scales above, write **I** below each TONIC, **IV** below each SUBDOMINANT and **VI** below each SUBMEDIANT.

Modern Sounds

This piece begins with the RH and LH moving up and down the keyboard in thirds. All the thirds are fingered with the 2nd and 4th fingers. RH and LH 2s are on neighboring white keys.

In the second section only the RH plays thirds. The LH plays fifths with 5 and 1.

STARTING POSITION

KEY OF C MAJOR
Key Signature: no ♯, no ♭.

*This piece combines the use of the relative minor and major keys.

D. C. al Fine

JAZZ SEQUENCES*

Willard A. Palmer

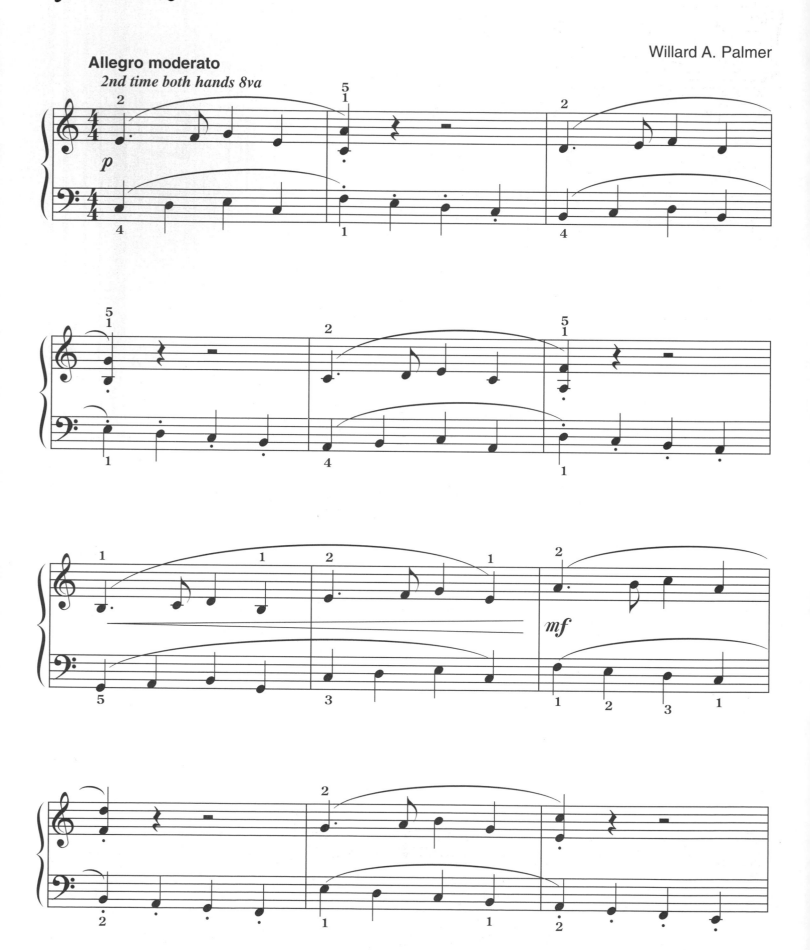

*The repetition of a musical pattern, beginning on a higher or lower note, is called a *sequence*.

D. C. al ⊕, then play CODA*

⊕ CODA

Both hands 8va ‒ ‒ ‒ ¬ loco

ritardando

pp

*Go back to the beginning and play to the sign ⊕; then play the CODA.

More Scale Degrees: Supertonic & Leading Tone

- The **SUPERTONIC** is the 2nd degree *above* the TONIC.
- The **LEADING TONE** is the 2nd degree *below* the TONIC.

The LEADING TONE is sometimes called the SUBTONIC. "Leading tone" is most often used, since the note has a strong tendency to "lead" to the TONIC, as it does in an ascending scale.

NOTE: The SUPERTONIC is always a *whole* step above the tonic.
The LEADING TONE is always a *half* step below the tonic.

KEY OF C MAJOR

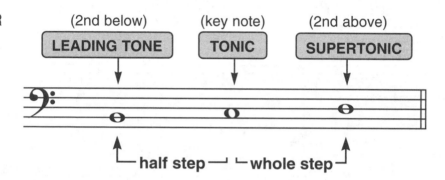

1. Write the LEADING TONE and SUPERTONIC degrees for each TONIC note:

KEY OF G MAJOR

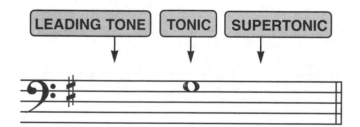

KEY OF D MAJOR

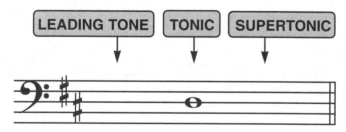

KEY OF F MAJOR

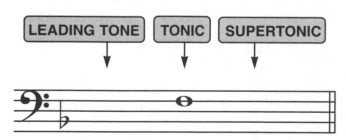

KEY OF B♭ MAJOR

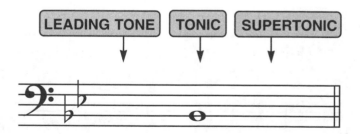

2. Write the answers in the blanks:

A is the LEADING TONE in the key of _____ major.
E is the LEADING TONE in the key of _____ major.

A is the SUPERTONIC in the key of _____ major.
E is the SUPERTONIC in the key of _____ major.

Writing the Supertonic & Leading Tone

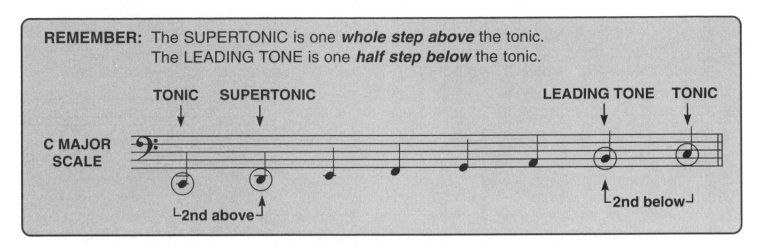

REMEMBER: The SUPERTONIC is one *whole step above* the tonic.
The LEADING TONE is one *half step below* the tonic.

In the scales below:
1. Circle all the TONIC notes.
2. Circle all the SUPERTONIC notes.
3. Circle all the LEADING TONES.

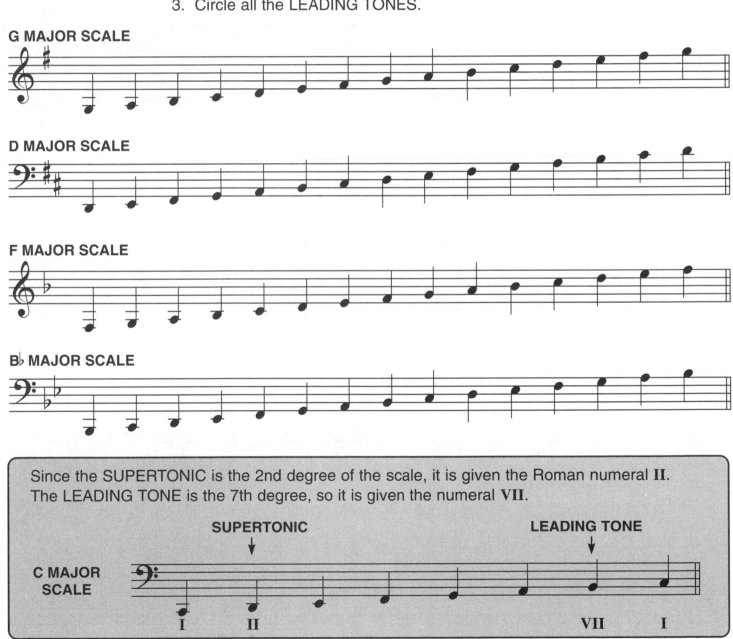

G MAJOR SCALE

D MAJOR SCALE

F MAJOR SCALE

B♭ MAJOR SCALE

Since the SUPERTONIC is the 2nd degree of the scale, it is given the Roman numeral **II**.
The LEADING TONE is the 7th degree, so it is given the numeral **VII**.

4. In the four scales above, write **I** below each TONIC, **II** below each SUPERTONIC
and **VII** below each LEADING TONE.

Reviewing the Scale Degrees

You now know the names of all the scale degrees. Arranged in order, the names are:

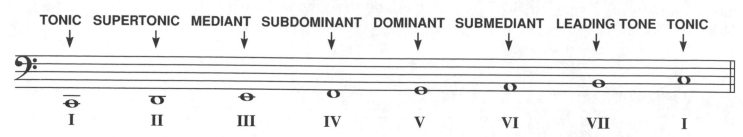

Be sure to remember that the degree names were derived from the following arrangement, in which the TONIC is taken as the center tone:

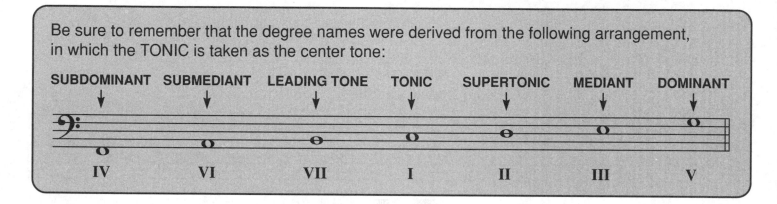

1. Write the degree names in the boxes above the notes.
2. Write the degree numbers (Roman numerals) in the boxes below the notes.

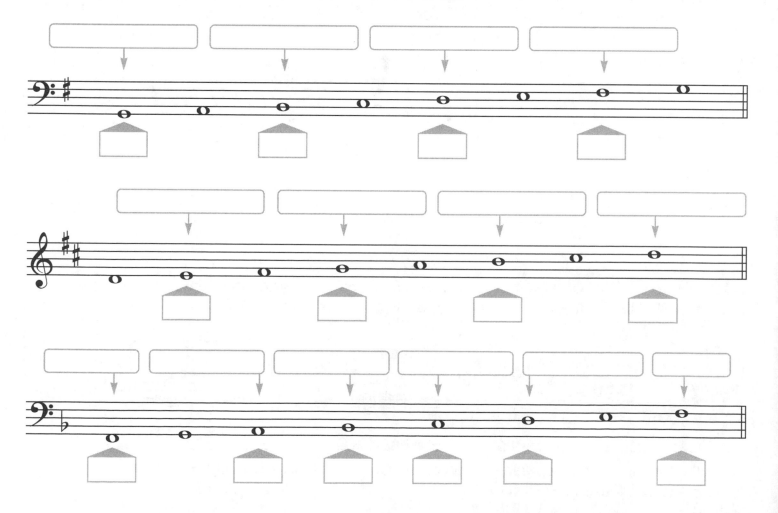

SCALE THE LADDERS!

If you know your scales, you should have no trouble going up and down these ladders. Begin with the Bb ladder (bottom left). To scale a ladder, simply write the name of each scale degree (tone) on each rung of the ladder. The starting rung is already filled in on each ladder. When you reach the top of the Bb ladder, continue: UP the F ladder, DOWN the C ladder, DOWN the G ladder, then UP the D ladder.

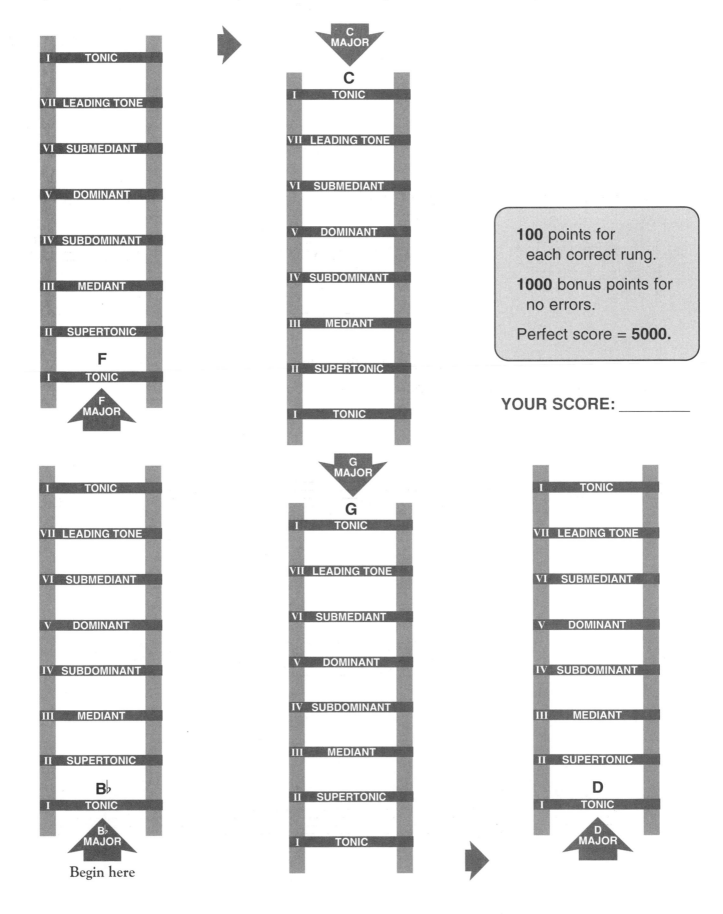

100 points for each correct rung.

1000 bonus points for no errors.

Perfect score = **5000.**

YOUR SCORE: _____

Alberti Bass

This style of LH accompaniment takes its name from the 18th-century Italian composer, Domenico Alberti, who used it extensively in his keyboard music. It consists of broken chords played in the following style, and it was frequently used by almost all the "classical" composers, including Haydn, Mozart, Clementi and Beethoven.

The first line of the music below shows a basic **I–IV–V^7** progression. The second and third lines introduce the corresponding Alberti bass in $\frac{4}{4}$ and $\frac{3}{4}$ time.

Play the following several times:

Alberti bass in $\frac{4}{4}$ time

Alberti bass in $\frac{3}{4}$ time

G MAJOR PROGRESSION

Write in the missing measures of Alberti bass, then play several times:

Alberti bass in $\frac{4}{4}$ time

Alberti bass in $\frac{3}{4}$ time

Alberti Bass in 4/4 Time in C Major

1. Write in the missing Alberti bass in 4/4 time.
2. Play, carefully observing phrasing and dynamics.

*When one slur ends where a new slur begins, it is called an ELISION. While there is no actual break between the two slurs, the notes at the end of the first group of slurred notes are usually tapered off (gradually softened) to the end of the phrase.

SERENADE from String Quartet, Op. 3, No. 5

Play the eighth notes *evenly!*

Franz Joseph Haydn

*OPTIONAL: The LH may be played one octave higher in the first and second lines.

When doing so, play the RH G half note (measure 4) as an eighth note.

28

THE GRAND PIANO BAND

JUST FOR FUN

March tempo
Eighths and quarters detached except where slurred.

Willard A. Palmer

*Play all eighth notes *evenly!*

A New Style of Bass

This style of accompaniment is often used in popular as well as classical music.
Begin with this as a warm-up:

Play the following exactly the same as the above, but HOLD the first note of each group of four notes:

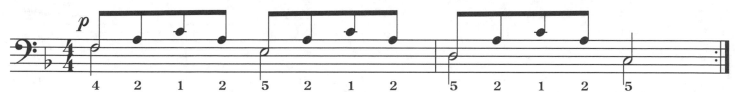

A VERY SPECIAL DAY

KEY OF F MAJOR
Key Signature: 1 flat (B♭)

Willard A. Palmer

1. This is a
ver - y spe - cial day   I'm of - fer - ing to   you,
ver - y spe - cial day   I'd love for you to   share.

The day I   dream of when I   pray   That wish - es may come
It's such a   ver - y spe - cial way   To show how much we

*ritardando and diminuendo

The Diminished Seventh Chord

The DIMINISHED SEVENTH chord may be formed by lowering each note of the DOMINANT SEVENTH (V^7) chord one half step, except the root, which remains the same.

IMPORTANT! The interval between each note of a diminished seventh chord is a *minor* 3rd (3 half steps)!

Be sure to *spell* each chord correctly! The Gdim7 chord must not be spelled **G B♭ D♭ E**, even though the notes E and F♭ are ENHARMONIC (that is, they represent the same key on the piano). The interval from G to E is a 6th. The interval from G to F♭ is a 7th (in this case a *diminished* 7th).

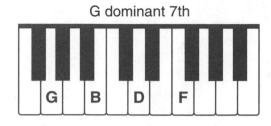

G dominant 7th

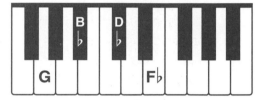

G diminished 7th (Gdim7)

In forming a Cdim7 chord, it is necessary to flat the note B♭. When a flatted note is flatted again, it becomes a DOUBLE FLAT, indicated by the sign ♭♭. In this case, the note must be called B♭♭, not A!

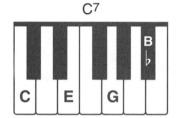

C7

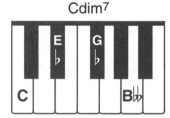

Cdim7

REMEMBER: When diminished 7th chords are properly spelled, one letter of the musical alphabet is skipped between each note. Use your SEVENTH CHORD VOCABULARY (Adult All-In-One Course, Level 2, page 92).

Play a dim7 chord on each note of the CHROMATIC SCALE, beginning as shown below. Build each chord by adding 3 notes above the root, each 3 half steps apart. Play with RH using 1 2 3 5 on each chord. Repeat one octave lower with LH, using 5 3 2 1.

A Classy Rag

Circle all the broken diminished 7th chords before you play.

*OPTIONAL: Play the *Introduction* with both hands *8va* as an added ending (CODA) for the entire piece.

Writing Diminished Seventh Chords

REMEMBER: The DIMINISHED SEVENTH chord may be formed by lowering each note of the DOMINANT SEVENTH (V⁷) chord one half step, except the root, which remains the same.

C dominant 7th (C7)

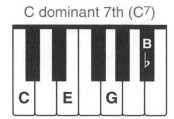

C diminished 7th (Cdim7)

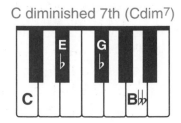

(add the missing accidentals)

1. In this exercise, the chords in the DOMINANT 7th column are spelled correctly. Chords in the DIMINISHED 7th column are not. Change each dominant 7th chord into a diminished 7th chord by lowering the 3rd, 5th and 7th of the chord in the diminished 7th column. Use naturals, flats and double flats. Each chord note *must* skip one letter of the musical alphabet.

   Remember: The double flat (♭♭) lowers a note ONE WHOLE STEP!

Dominant 7ths				Diminished 7ths			
Root	3rd	5th	7th	Root	3rd	5th	7th
D	F♯	A	C	D	F	A	C
G	B	D	F	G	B	D	F
C	E	G	B♭	C	E	G	B
F	A	C	E♭	F	A	C	E
B♭	D	F	A♭	B♭	D	F	A
E♭	G	B♭	D♭	E♭	G	B	D
A♭	C	E♭	G♭	A♭	C	E	G

2. Play each DOMINANT 7th above, followed by the DIMINISHED 7th in the column on the right. Use RH 1 2 3 5 or LH 5 3 2 1, saying the name of each chord as you play it:

   "G dominant 7th, G diminished 7th," *etc.*

A DIMINISHED SEVENTH chord may also be formed on any given root by stacking intervals of a *minor 3rd* (3 half steps) above it. (See page 35).

---

3. Play the following diminished 7th chords, using RH 1 2 3 5.
   Check each chord to be sure that the interval between each note is a *minor 3rd.*

An Easy Way to Make ANY Diminished Seventh Chord

Here is a quick and easy way to make *any* DIMINISHED 7th chord:

> Choose any note as the root.
> Go up **3 half steps** for the **3rd.**
> Go up **3 half steps** again for the **5th.**
> Go up **3 half steps** again for the **7th.**

EXAMPLE: G dim 7th

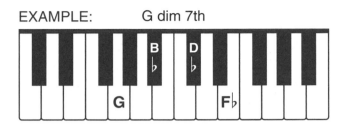

1. Play each of the following DIMINISHED 7th chords in several places on the keyboard. Use **RH 1 2 3 5.** Repeat, using **LH 5 3 2 1.** Carefully note that there are exactly **3 half steps** between each of the four notes of each chord.

A dim 7th

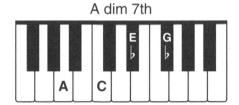

E dim 7th

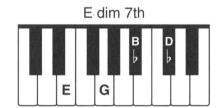

B dim 7th

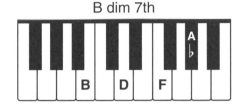

2. Build diminished 7th chords on each of the following keyboard diagrams, using the given note as the ROOT of the chord. Write the letter names of the **3rd, 5th** and **7th** on each keyboard.

   To be sure you are spelling each chord correctly, use the SEVENTH CHORD VOCABULARY (Adult All-In-One Course, Level 2, page 92).

REMEMBER: Each chord note must skip one letter of the musical alphabet.

F dim 7th

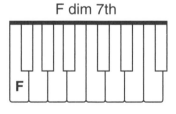

F# dim 7th

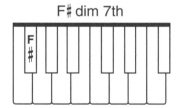

G dim 7th

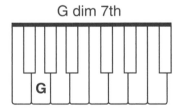

C dim 7th

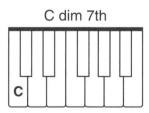

C# dim 7th

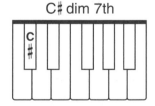

D dim 7th

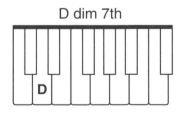

B♭ dim 7th

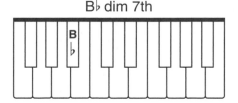

E♭ dim 7th

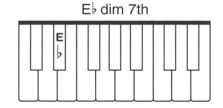

G# dim 7th

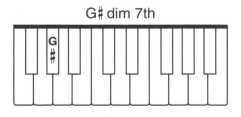

A Special Style of Pedaling

In the following piece, the pedal is applied only to the eighth notes played by the RH. These notes should be played with a clear legato touch, even though they are sustained by the pedal.

Observance of the two-part writing in the left hand results in the sustaining of the LH notes with the *fingers.* This is sometimes called *finger pedaling.* By combining LH finger pedaling with pedaled notes in the RH, a beautiful tone color is produced. This style of pedaling is often effective, especially in pieces constructed largely of broken-chord figurations.

PRELUDE IN D MINOR

KEY OF D MINOR*
Key Signature: 1 flat (B♭)

Muzio Clementi
from *Introduction to the Art
of Playing on the Pianoforte*

*REMINDER: D MINOR is the *relative minor* of the key of F MAJOR.

How many broken diminished 7th chords can you find in this piece?
Check the spelling of each diminished 7th chord.

NOTE: You may now wish to play *PRELUDE IN C MAJOR,* from J. S. Bach's *Well Tempered Clavier, Vol. 1,* found on pages 122–125, in the "AMBITIOUS" section of this book. The Bach prelude is especially effective when you use the same style of pedaling as is mentioned above.

THE STAR-SPANGLED BANNER

KEY OF B♭ MAJOR
Key Signature: 2 flats (B♭ & E♭)

Words by Francis Scott Key
Music by John Stafford Smith

Con spirito*

Con spirito means "with spirit."

rock - et's red glare, The bombs burst - ing in air, gave

proof through the night that our flag was still there. **Slower** Oh,

f say does that Star - Span - gled Ban - ner yet wave, O'er the

land of the free and the home of the *ritardando* brave?

* This sign means *tremolo*. Alternate the lower and upper note of the octave as rapidly as you can, keeping the wrist relaxed. (You may also just play the octave and hold it for the entire measure.)

Reviewing: Major & Minor Triads

You have learned to identify MAJOR and MINOR triads in ROOT POSITION as follows:

- MAJOR triads consist of a MAJOR 3rd and a PERFECT 5th. ⎫
- MINOR triads consist of a MINOR 3rd and a PERFECT 5th. ⎬ **Intervals above the root**

You may also consider these triads as consisting of "stacked 3rds":

- MAJOR triads consist of a MAJOR 3rd plus a MINOR 3rd. ⎫
- MINOR triads consist of a MINOR 3rd plus a MAJOR 3rd. ⎬ **Intervals from note to note**

> **REMEMBER:** a MAJOR 3rd has 4 half steps; a MINOR 3rd has 3 half steps.

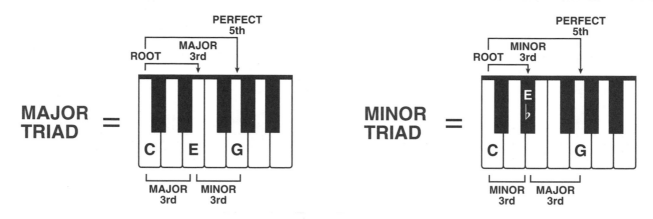

1. In the box below each diagram, write "MAJOR" for each major triad, and "MINOR" for each minor triad, as shown in the first example.

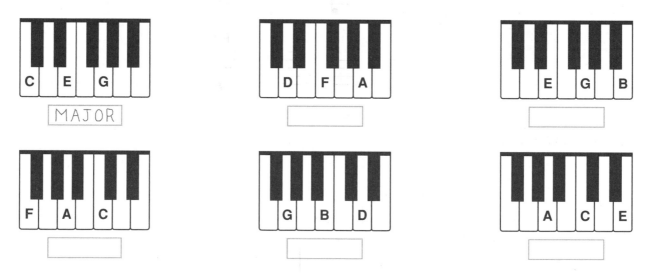

Triads Built on the First Six Degrees of the C Major Scale

2. In the box just below the name of each scale degree, write "MAJOR" if the triad is major, or "MINOR" if the triad is minor.

3. In the lower row of boxes write the Roman numerals for each scale degree.
   (Use upper case numerals for major; lower case for minor.)

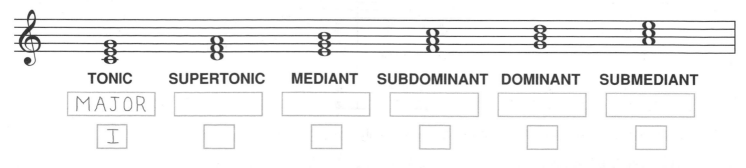

MAKE UP YOUR MIND!

*The pairs of eighth notes may be played a bit unevenly (long-short).

42

Scene from the Ballet, "Swan Lake"

Peter Ilyich Tchaikovsky (1840–1893) was a great Russian composer who found success in every musical medium, including symphonies, songs, opera, chamber music, instrumental and choral works, and ballet. There is no more popular large piano work than his famous *Concerto in B♭ Minor,* which American pianist Van Cliburn played when he won the International Piano Competition in Moscow in 1957. Tchaikovsky also gave the world its two most famous ballets: *The Nutcracker,* and *Swan Lake,* from which this scene is taken.

Tchaikovsky
adapted by P. M. L.

KEY OF G MINOR*
Key Signature: 2 flats (B♭ & E♭)

*REMINDER: G MINOR is the *relative minor* of the key of B♭ MAJOR.

meno mosso means "slower."

SCHEHERAZADE

Theme from the Third Movement
"THE YOUNG PRINCE AND THE YOUNG PRINCESS"

N. Rimsky-Korsakov

KEY OF G MAJOR
Key Signature: 1 sharp (F♯)

*Slide the thumb from D♯ to E, as smoothly as possible.

Poco meno mosso

Tempo primo**
8va -

*The three notes of a sixteenth note triplet are played evenly, in the time of *one eighth note.*

Tempo primo means "the first tempo," in this case, **andante.**

Preparation: Play several times, counting aloud.

THEME FROM "THE UNFINISHED SYMPHONY"

Franz Schubert

Moderato

*Play the C & D together with the side tip of the thumb.

*REMINDER: *sf* (sforzando)* means suddenly louder on one note or chord. Here it applies to both RH and LH notes.

**OPTIONAL: You may play octaves in place of the tremolo, using half notes.

48

SPOOKY STORY

KEY OF E MINOR*
Key Signature: 1 sharp (F♯)

Andante moderato, mysteriously

VERY IMPORTANT: Play both hands one octave lower than written throughout!

Fine

***REMINDER:** E MINOR is the *relative minor* of the key of G MAJOR.

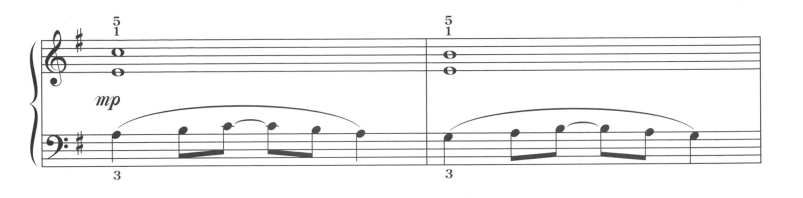

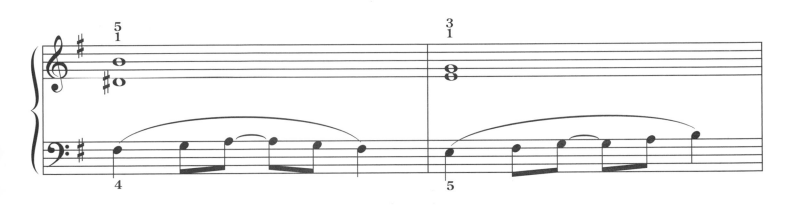

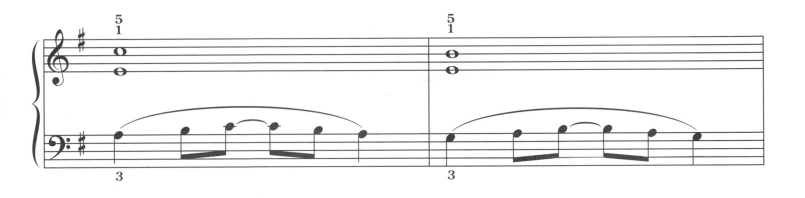

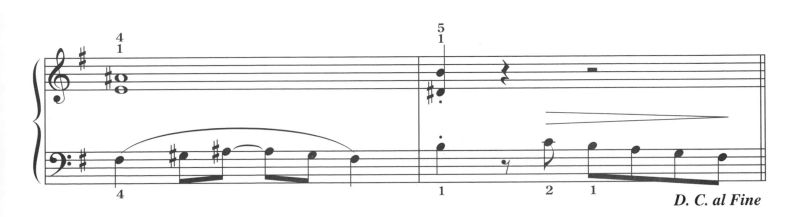

D. C. al Fine

STEAL AWAY

KEY OF D MAJOR
Key Signature: 2 sharps (F♯ & C♯)

Adagio moderato

Spiritual

This popular Neapolitan song has been a favorite selection for famous tenor soloists since the time of Caruso. It is often performed by Placido Domingo and Luciano Pavarotti.

COME BACK TO SORRENTO

Ernesto de Curtis

*Some pieces combine a minor key and its parallel major key. Parallel keys have the same *key-note*.
D minor and D major are *parallel* keys.

NOTE: You may now play Jeremiah Clarke's famous *TRUMPET TUNE,* on page 126 in the "AMBITIOUS" section of this book, if you wish!

Arpeggios

The word *arpeggio* comes from the Italian *arpeggiare,* which means "to play upon a harp." This refers to playing the notes of a chord in a broken fashion, one after another, as one does when playing a harp.

In the next to last measure of *A VERY SPECIAL DAY* (page 31), you played an arpeggio through 3 octaves, dividing the chords between the hands. Now you will learn to play arpeggios through several octaves using only one hand.

Turn the wrists slightly outward. After the thumb plays, carry it at the base of the 3rd finger, and let the *arm* carry it to its new position in the next octave. Keep the wrist quiet.

RH PREPARATION   Practice very slowly at first.

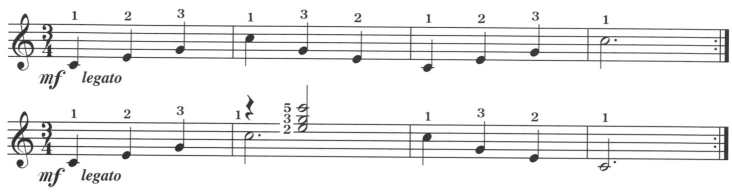

RH TWO-OCTAVE ARPEGGIO

LH PREPARATION   Practice very slowly at first.

LH TWO-OCTAVE ARPEGGIO

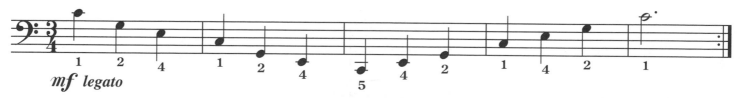

You are now ready to play arpeggios on the following triads:

C MAJOR, D MINOR, E MINOR, F MAJOR, G MAJOR and A MINOR.

These arpeggios are all fingered the same.

MAGIC CARPET RIDE

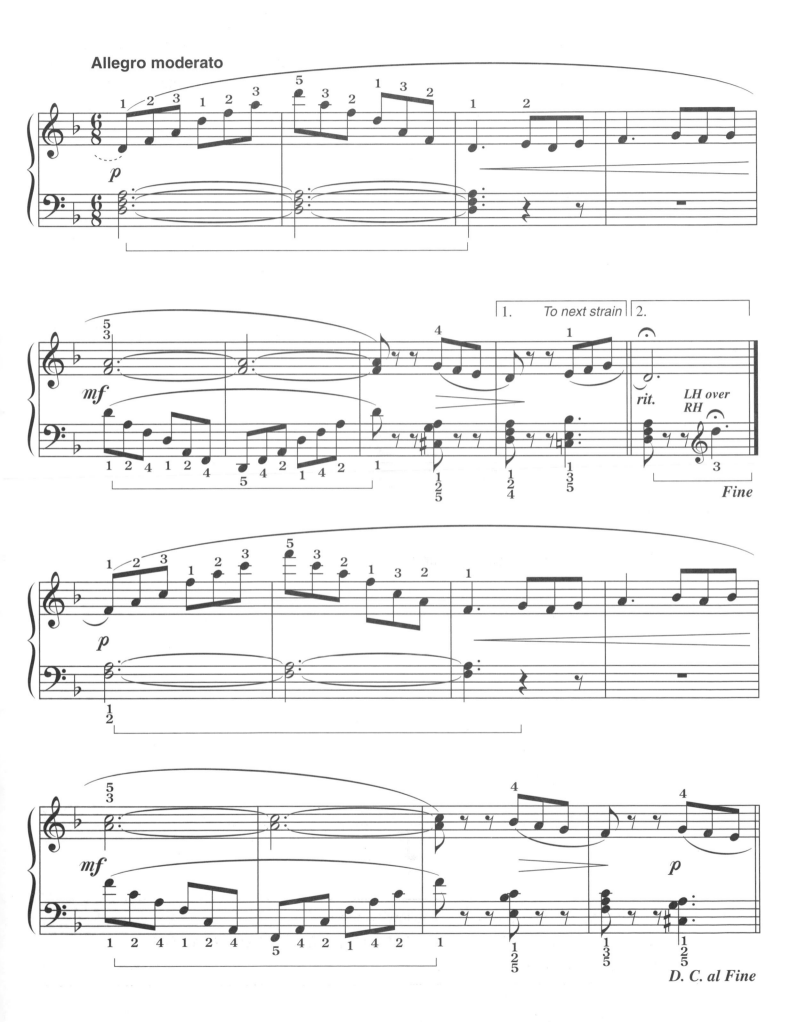

D. C. al Fine

IN THE HALL OF THE MOUNTAIN KING
from "Peer Gynt Suite"

KEY OF B MINOR*
Key Signature: 2 sharps (F♯ & C♯)

NOTE: This piece begins with *both* hands playing in bass clef!

Edvard Grieg

*REMINDER: B MINOR is the *relative minor* of the key of D MAJOR.

** *Alla marcia* means "march-like."

*Note the spelling of the diminished 7th chord: D E♯ G♯ B. This means that it is an inversion of the E♯dim7: E♯ G♯ B D. The correct spelling of any dim7 in root position skips one letter of the musical alphabet between each note.

The A Major Scale

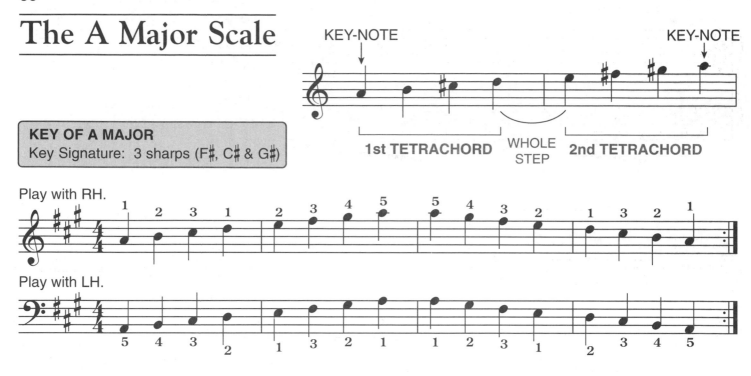

1st TETRACHORD **WHOLE STEP** **2nd TETRACHORD**

KEY OF A MAJOR
Key Signature: 3 sharps (F♯, C♯ & G♯)

Play with RH.

Play with LH.

THE A MAJOR SCALE IN CONTRARY MOTION

Practice this scale in parallel motion by playing the top two lines of this page with hands together.

An American Hymn

Many famous American composers, including Aaron Copland and Charles Ives, have made special arrangements of this 19th century hymn. This is a very quiet and contemplative setting.

Shall we gather at the river
Where bright angel feet have trod;
With its crystal tide forever
Flowing by the throne of God?

Yes, we'll gather at the river,
The beautiful, the beautiful river;
Gather with the saints at the river,
That flows by the throne of God.

Slowly and quietly

Robert Lowry

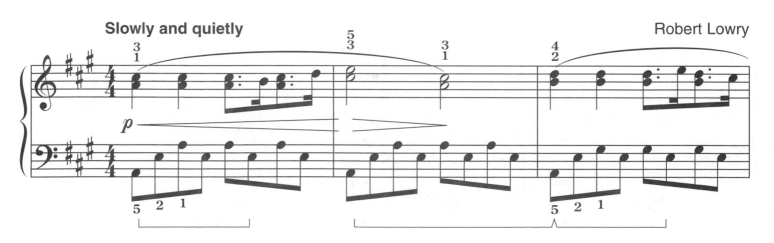

Writing the A Major Scale

1. Write the letter names of the notes of the A MAJOR SCALE, from *left* to *right*, on the keyboard below. Be sure the WHOLE STEPS & HALF STEPS are correct!

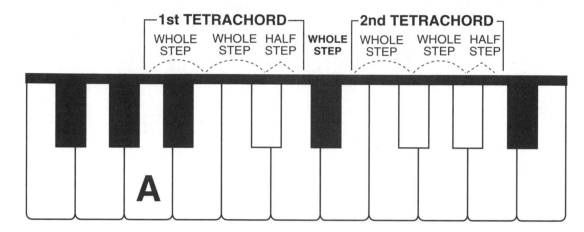

2. Check to be sure that you named the notes in the order of the musical alphabet. If you did, all the black keys will be named as *sharps,* not *flats.*

3. Complete the tetrachord beginning on A. Write one note over each finger number.

4. Complete the tetrachord beginning on E. Write one note over each finger number.

NOTE: The fingering for the A MAJOR SCALE is the same as for the C MAJOR, G MAJOR & D MAJOR SCALES.

4. Write the fingering UNDER each note of the following LH scale. Cross 3 over 1 ascending. Pass 1 under 3 descending.

5. Play with LH.

6. Write the fingering OVER each note of the following RH scale. Pass 1 under 3 ascending. Cross 3 over 1 descending.

7. Play with RH.

The Primary Chords in A Major

KEY OF A MAJOR
Key Signature: 3 sharps (F♯, C♯ & G♯)

In major keys, the **I** chord is the TONIC chord (major).
The **IV** chord is the SUBDOMINANT chord (major).
The **V⁷** chord is the DOMINANT 7th chord.

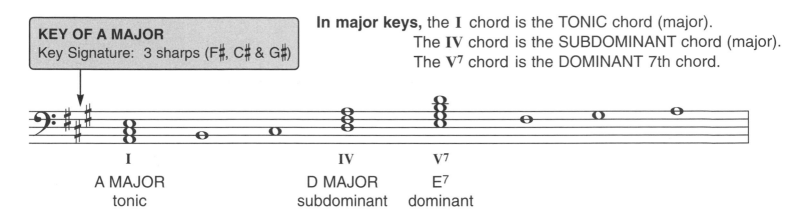

I	IV	V⁷
A MAJOR	D MAJOR	E⁷
tonic	subdominant	dominant

The following positions are often used for smooth progressions:

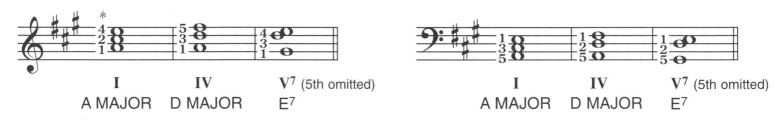

I	IV	V⁷ (5th omitted)		I	IV	V⁷ (5th omitted)
A MAJOR	D MAJOR	E⁷		A MAJOR	D MAJOR	E⁷

1. Add the A MAJOR key signature to each staff below.
2. Write the PRIMARY CHORDS in A MAJOR, using the above positions.

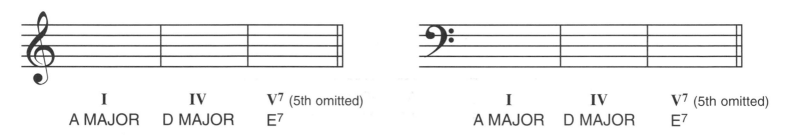

I	IV	V⁷ (5th omitted)		I	IV	V⁷ (5th omitted)
A MAJOR	D MAJOR	E⁷		A MAJOR	D MAJOR	E⁷

3. Write the ROMAN NUMERALS (**I, IV, V⁷**) in the boxes below.
4. Play.

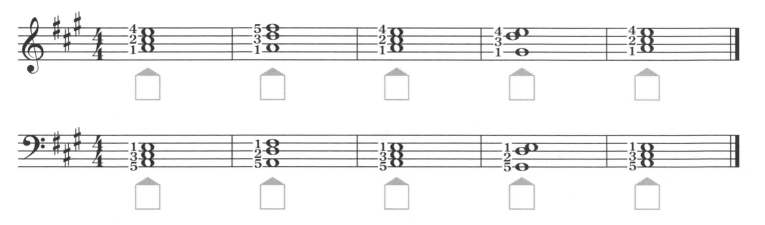

*Fingering for chords varies depending on the context of the chord. 1 2 4 is used here for the A major triad
because it allows a smooth progression to the next chord.

62

The Primary Chords in A Major—All Positions

1. In the blank measures after each ROOT POSITION chord, write the two INVERSIONS of the chord.

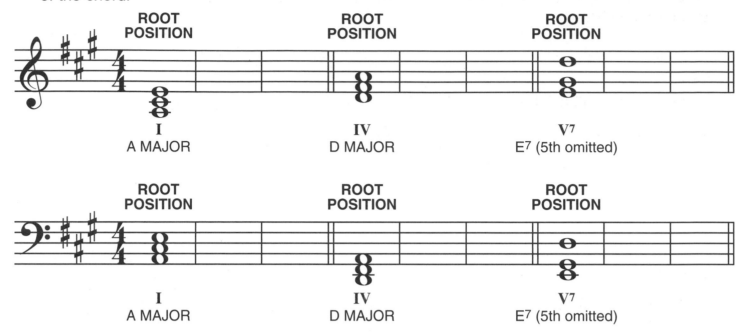

ROOT POSITION   ROOT POSITION   ROOT POSITION

I   IV   V7
A MAJOR   D MAJOR   E7 (5th omitted)

ROOT POSITION   ROOT POSITION   ROOT POSITION

I   IV   V7
A MAJOR   D MAJOR   E7 (5th omitted)

2. On the two keyboards to the right of each ROOT POSITION chord, write the letter names showing the two inversions of the chord.

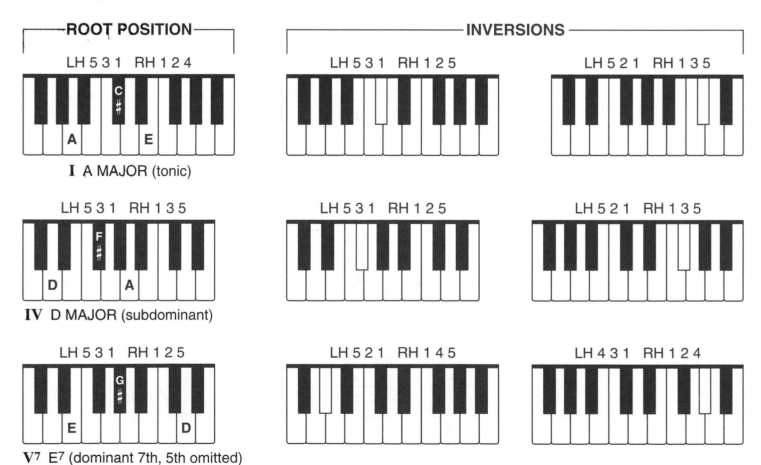

3. Play each chord shown on the above keyboards in any convenient place on your piano, first with LH, then with RH. Use the fingering shown above each keyboard.

More Minors, Majors & Arpeggios

- Any MINOR TRIAD may be changed to a MAJOR TRIAD by raising the 3rd one half step!
- When the triad is in ROOT POSITION, you simply add an accidental before the MIDDLE NOTE to raise it one half step.

1. Change each of the following MINOR triads to MAJOR triads by adding an accidental before the MIDDLE note to raise it one half step.

2. Write the name of each triad (after you have changed it) in the box below it.

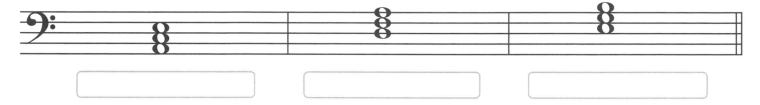

The only MAJOR triads that have *white keys* for the root and fifth, and a *black key* for the third are the following:

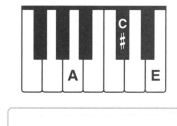 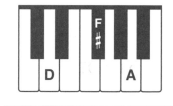 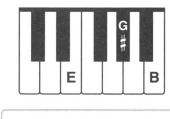

3. Write the name of each of the above triads in the box below it.

Two-octave arpeggios on the A MAJOR, D MAJOR & E MAJOR triads are fingered the same.
Notice that with the RH, the 2nd finger is used on the black keys; with LH, the 3rd.

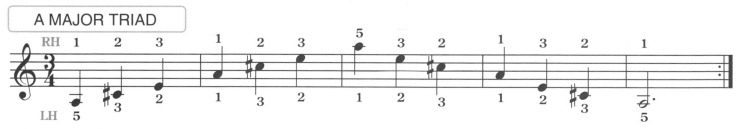

4. Write the name of the arpeggiated triad in the box at the beginning of each staff below.
5. Write the RH fingering ABOVE each note.
6. Write the LH fingering BELOW each note.
7. Play with RH as written.
8. Play with LH two octaves lower than written.

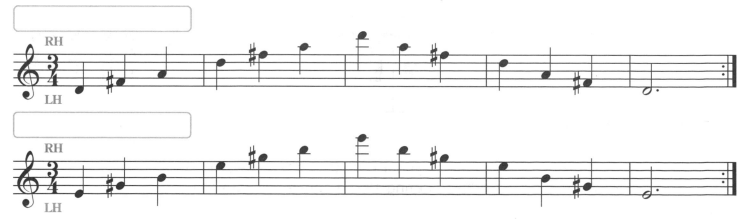

ADAGIO IN A MAJOR

This expressive piece is excellent preparation for the Chopin *PRELUDE IN A MAJOR,* found in the **"AMBITIOUS"** section on page 137.

Alexander Morovsky

* // = Caesura or pause.

The Key of F♯ Minor (Relative of A Major)

F♯ MINOR is the relative of A MAJOR. Both keys have the same key signature (3 sharps, F♯, C♯ & G♯).

THE F♯ HARMONIC MINOR SCALE

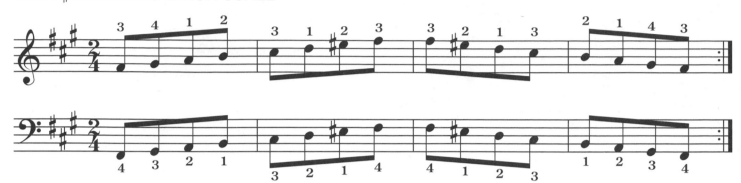

THE F♯ HARMONIC MINOR SCALE IN CONTRARY MOTION

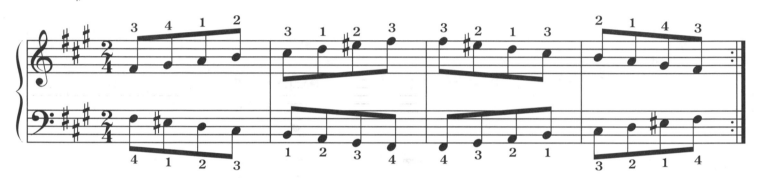

Practice this scale in parallel motion by playing the top two lines of this page with hands together.

The NATURAL & MELODIC MINOR scales may also be practiced in parallel and contrary motion.

• The NATURAL MINOR scale uses only the sharps in the key signature (no E♯).

• The MELODIC MINOR scale adds D♯ and E♯ ascending.
  The RH ascending fingering is 3 4 1 2 3 4 1 3. It descends like the natural minor.

BLUE RONDO*

Moderate blues tempo

Section Ⓐ

*A **rondo** has at least three sections. The first section is repeated after each of the other sections, and there is often a *CODA* (added ending).

Section Ⓑ

Section Ⓐ

Section C

Section A

Coda

The last two chords may be played with *tremolo:*

Scales in F♯ Minor

REMEMBER: The RELATIVE MINOR begins on the 6th tone of the MAJOR SCALE.

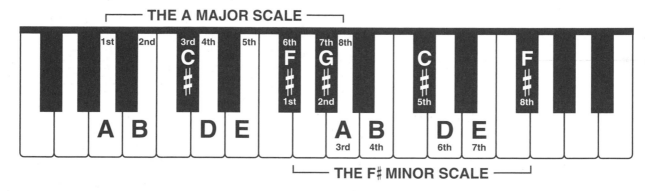

There are *three* kinds of minor scales: the natural, the harmonic, and the melodic.

THE NATURAL MINOR SCALE: This scale uses *only* the tones of the relative major scale.

1. Play with hands separate, then together.

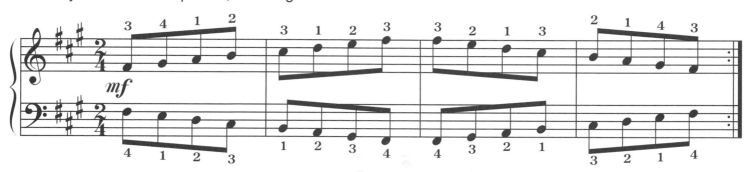

THE HARMONIC MINOR SCALE: The 7th tone (E) is raised 1 half step (to E♯), ascending & descending.

2. Add accidentals needed to change these NATURAL minor scales into HARMONIC minor scales.
3. Play with hands separate, then together.

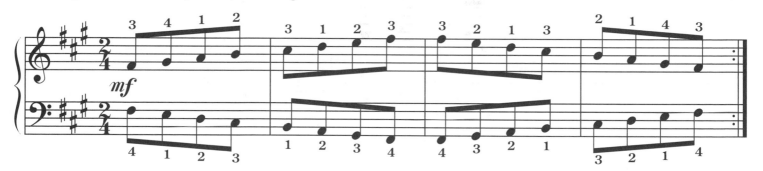

THE MELODIC MINOR SCALE: 6th (D) and 7th (E) raised 1 half step (to D♯ & E♯) ASCENDING; DESCENDS like natural minor.

4. Add accidentals needed to change these NATURAL minor scales into MELODIC minor scales.
5. Play with hands separate.   6. (OPTIONAL) Play with hands together.

Note that the RH fingering for the MELODIC minor scale differs from the two other minor scales. It is played this way to avoid using the thumb on the raised 6th (D♯).

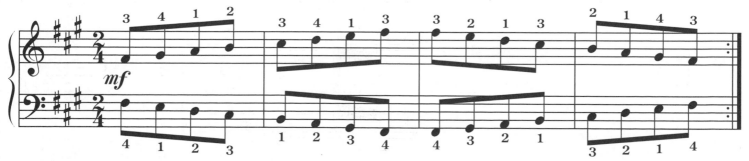

The Primary Chords in F# Minor

REMEMBER: In **MINOR** keys, the **i** chord is the TONIC chord (minor).
The **iv** chord is the SUBDOMINANT chord (minor).
The **V⁷** chord is the DOMINANT 7th chord.

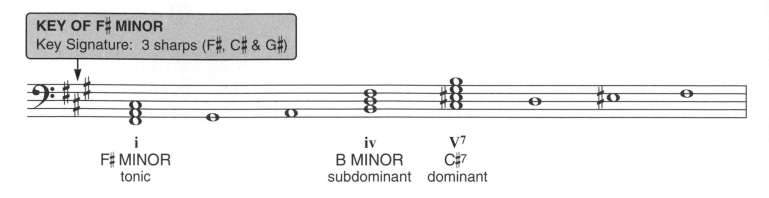

KEY OF F# MINOR
Key Signature: 3 sharps (F#, C# & G#)

i — F# MINOR — tonic
iv — B MINOR — subdominant
V⁷ — C#⁷ — dominant

The following positions are often used for smooth progressions:

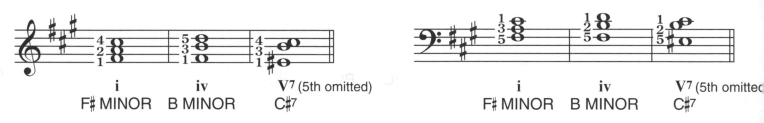

i — F# MINOR
iv — B MINOR
V⁷ (5th omitted) — C#⁷

1. Add the F# MINOR key signature to each staff below.
2. Write the PRIMARY CHORDS in the key of F# MINOR, using the above positions.

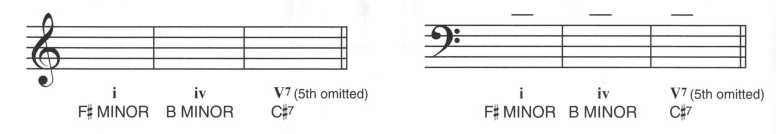

i — F# MINOR
iv — B MINOR
V⁷ (5th omitted) — C#⁷

i — F# MINOR
iv — B MINOR
V⁷ (5th omitted) — C#⁷

3. Write the ROMAN NUMERALS (**i**, **iv**, **V⁷**) in the boxes below.
4. Play.

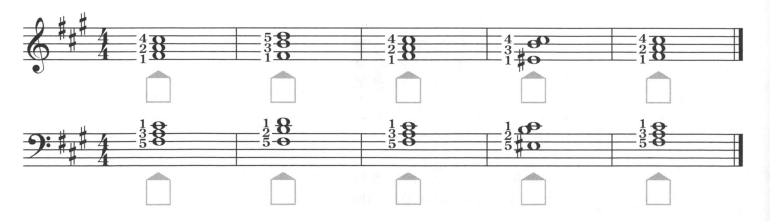

The Primary Chords in F♯ Minor—All Positions

1. In the blank measures after each ROOT POSITION chord, write the two INVERSIONS of the chord.

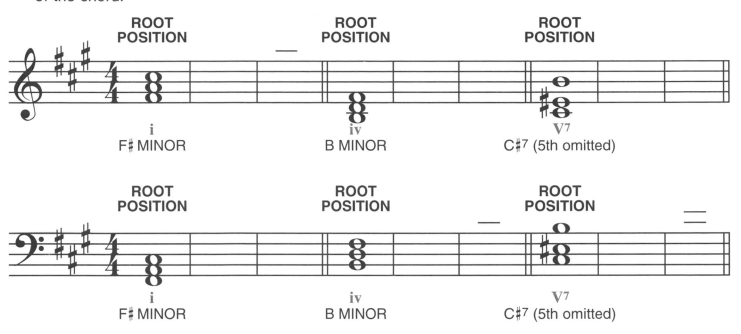

ROOT POSITION	ROOT POSITION	ROOT POSITION
i F♯ MINOR	iv B MINOR	V7 C♯7 (5th omitted)

ROOT POSITION	ROOT POSITION	ROOT POSITION
i F♯ MINOR	iv B MINOR	V7 C♯7 (5th omitted)

2. On the two keyboards to the right of each ROOT POSITION chord, write the letter names showing the two inversions of the chord.

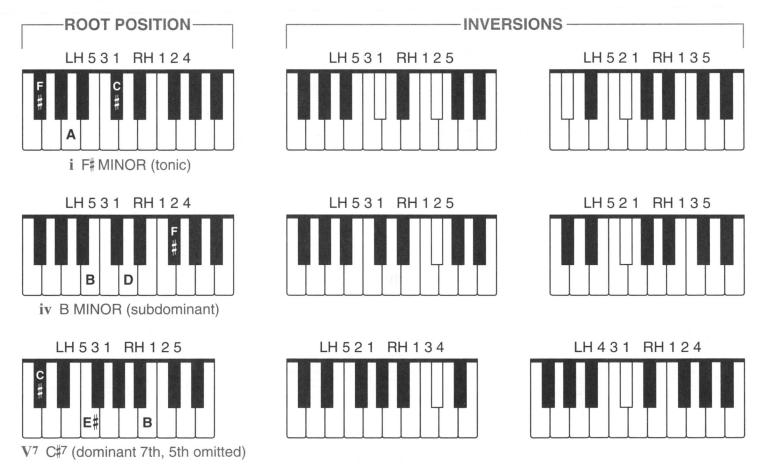

ROOT POSITION — INVERSIONS

LH 5 3 1 RH 1 2 4
i F♯ MINOR (tonic)

LH 5 3 1 RH 1 2 4
iv B MINOR (subdominant)

LH 5 3 1 RH 1 2 5
V7 C♯7 (dominant 7th, 5th omitted)

3. Play each chord shown on the above keyboards in any convenient place on your piano, first with LH, then with RH. Use the fingering shown above each keyboard.

JUST A "GOOD OLD TUNE"

JUST FOR FUN

Happily
2nd time only, play both hands 8va

Willard A. Palmer

*This piece is effective with eighth notes played evenly or with a slight lilt, *long-short*.

CODA Both hands 8va 1st time
      Both hands loco 2nd time

Not a toc-ca - ta,   not a so-na - ta,   Just a good old   tune! (Once more!)*   tune!

*Spoken: "Once more!"

The E Major Scale

KEY-NOTE   KEY-NOTE

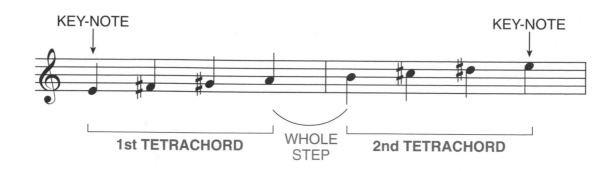

1st TETRACHORD   WHOLE STEP   2nd TETRACHORD

> **KEY OF E MAJOR**
> Key Signature: 4 sharps (F♯, C♯, G♯ & D♯)

Play with RH.

Play with LH.

THE E MAJOR SCALE IN CONTRARY MOTION

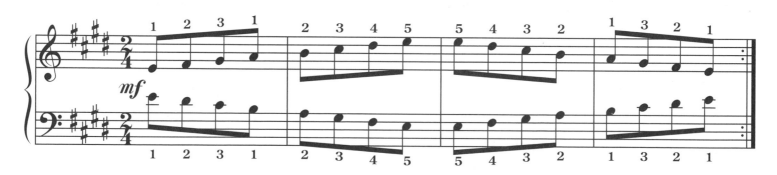

Practice this scale in parallel motion by playing the top two lines of this page with hands together.

LH Warm-up for *SHENANDOAH*
Play several times.

SHENANDOAH

American Folk Song

Writing the E Major Scale

1. Write the letter names of the notes of the E MAJOR SCALE, from *left* to *right,*
   on the keyboard below. Be sure the WHOLE STEPS & HALF STEPS are correct!

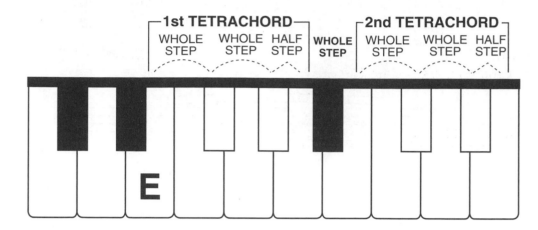

2. Check to be sure that you named the notes in the order of the musical alphabet.
   If you did, all the black keys will be named as *sharps,* not *flats.*

3. Complete the tetrachord beginning on E.   4. Complete the tetrachord beginning on B.
   Write one note over each finger number.   Write one note over each finger number.

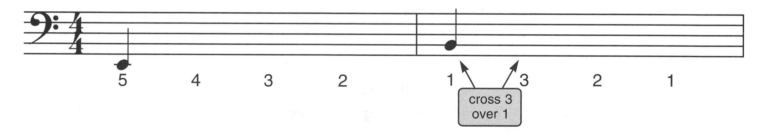

> **NOTE:**   The fingering for the E MAJOR SCALE is the same as for the
>   C MAJOR, G MAJOR, D MAJOR & A MAJOR SCALES.

4. Write the fingering UNDER each note of the following LH scale.
   Cross 3 over 1 ascending. Pass 1 under 3 descending.

5. Play with LH.

7. Write the fingering OVER each note of the following RH scale.
   Pass 1 under 3 ascending. Cross 3 over 1 descending.

8. Play with RH.

The Primary Chords in E Major

REMEMBER: **In MAJOR keys,** the **I** chord is the TONIC chord (major).
The **IV** chord is the SUBDOMINANT chord (major).
The **V⁷** chord is the DOMINANT 7th chord.

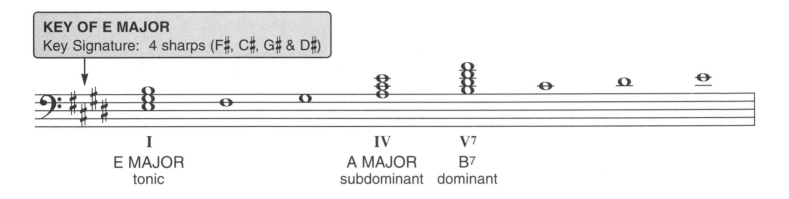

The following positions are often used for smooth progressions:

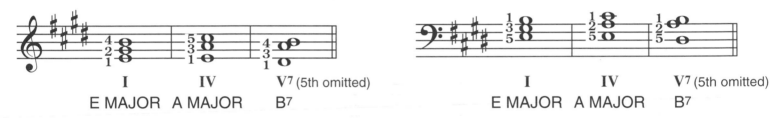

1. Add the E MAJOR key signature to each staff below.
2. Write the PRIMARY CHORDS in E MAJOR, using the above positions.

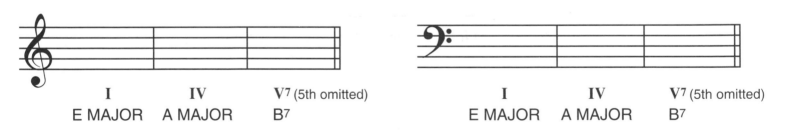

3. Write the ROMAN NUMERALS (**I**, **IV**, **V⁷**) in the boxes below.
4. Play.

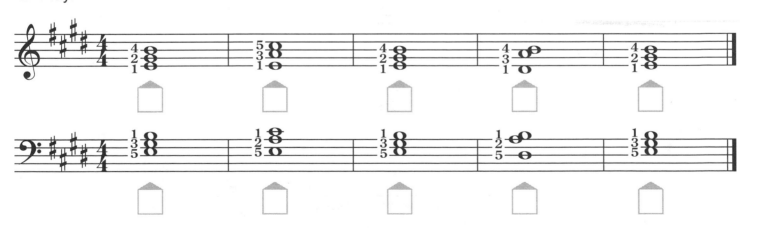

LAREDO

This favorite Mexican folk song was used by the great American composer, Aaron Copland, as one of the themes in his famous symphonic composition, *El Salón Mexico.*

Traditional

Andante moderato

* ✖ Double sharp raises a sharped note one *half step,* or a natural note one *whole step.*

The Primary Chords in E Major—All Positions

1. In the blank measures after each ROOT POSITION chord, write the two INVERSIONS of the chord.

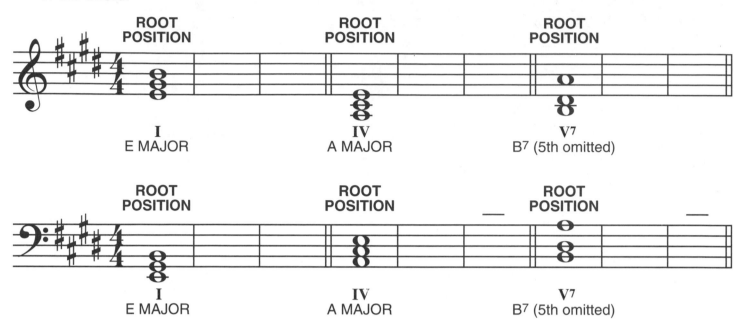

2. On the two keyboards to the right of each ROOT POSITION chord, write the letter names showing the two inversions of the chord.

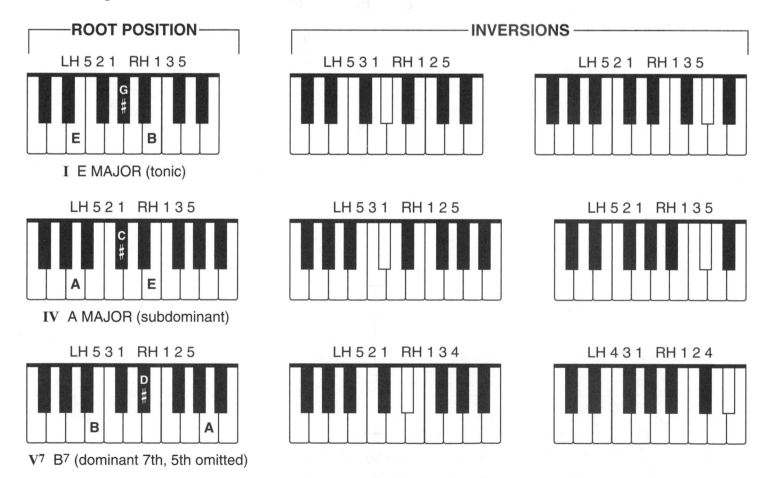

3. Play each chord shown on the above keyboards in any convenient place on your piano, first with LH, then with RH. Use the fingering shown above each keyboard.

Completing the Circle of 5ths (sharps)

THE SHARP KEY SIGNATURES

Beginning with C and moving upward in 5ths clockwise, the order of keys around the circle is

C G D A E B F♯ C♯

Each key has one more sharp than the previous one, as you move around the circle clockwise.

The key of C MAJOR has no sharps.

The key of G MAJOR has 1 sharp (F♯).

The key of D MAJOR has 2 sharps (F♯ & C♯), *etc.,* continuing around the circle until all the notes are sharp.

The key of C♯ MAJOR has 7 sharps: (F♯, C♯, G♯, D♯, A♯, E♯ & B♯).

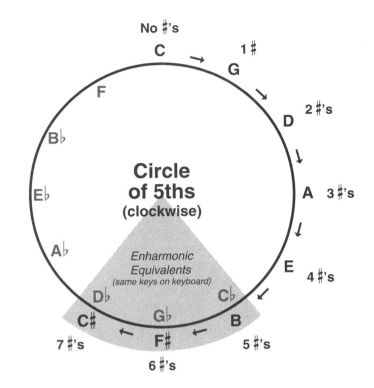

Copy the sharps of each key signature in the blank measure following it.

G MAJOR
1♯ (F♯)

D MAJOR
2♯'s (F♯, C♯)

A MAJOR
3♯'s (F♯, C♯, G♯)

E MAJOR
4♯'s (F♯, C♯, G♯, D♯)

B MAJOR
5♯'s (F♯, C♯, G♯, D♯, A♯)

F♯ MAJOR
6♯'s (F♯, C♯, G♯, D♯, A♯, E♯)

C♯ MAJOR
7♯'s (F♯, C♯, G♯, D♯, A♯, E♯, B♯)

IMPORTANT!   Notice that the sharps in the key signatures occur in the order of the letters (moving clockwise) around the Circle of 5ths, beginning with F.

F♯   C♯   G♯   D♯   A♯   E♯   B♯

The Key of C# Minor (Relative of E Major)

C# MINOR is the relative of E MAJOR.

Both keys have the same key signature (4 sharps, F#, C#, G# & D#).

THE C# HARMONIC MINOR SCALE

Play with RH.

Play with LH.

THE C# HARMONIC MINOR SCALE IN CONTRARY MOTION

Practice this scale in parallel motion by playing the top two lines of this page with hands together.

The NATURAL & MELODIC MINOR scales may also be practiced in parallel and contrary motion.

• The NATURAL MINOR scale uses only the sharps in the key signature (no B#).

• The MELODIC MINOR scale uses A# and B# ascending.
  The RH ascending fingering is 3 4 1 2 3 4 1 3. It descends like the natural minor.

Scales in C♯ Minor

REMEMBER: The RELATIVE MINOR begins on the 6th tone of the MAJOR SCALE.

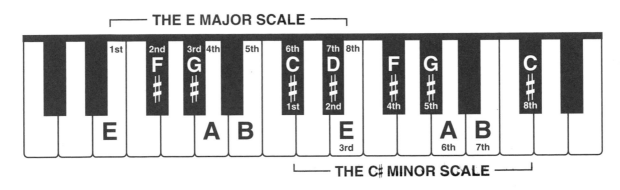

THE NATURAL MINOR SCALE: This scale uses *only* the tones of the relative major scale.

1. Play with hands separate, then together.

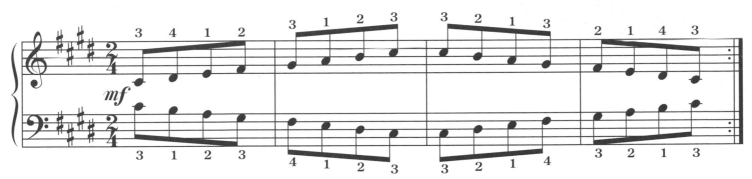

THE HARMONIC MINOR SCALE: The 7th tone (B) is raised 1 half step (to B♯), ascending & descending.

2. Add accidentals needed to change these NATURAL minor scales into HARMONIC minor scales.
3. Play with hands separate, then together.

THE MELODIC MINOR SCALE: 6th (A) and 7th (B) raised 1 half step (to A♯ & B♯) ASCENDING; DESCENDS like natural minor.

4. Add accidentals needed to change these NATURAL minor scales into MELODIC minor scales.
5. Play with hands separate.   6. (OPTIONAL) Play with hands together.

Note that the RH fingering for the MELODIC minor scale differs from the two other minor scales. It is played this way to avoid using the thumb on the raised 6th (A♯).

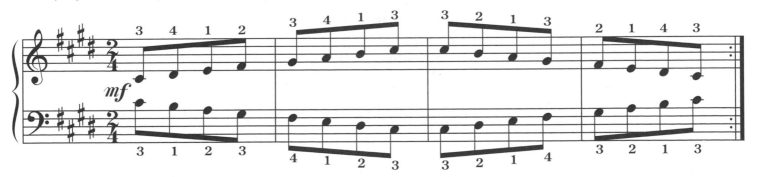

JAZZ OSTINATO* IN C♯ MINOR

This particular LH pattern is an excellent technical exercise!

Ostinato = Italian for "obstinate" or "persistent"; a pattern of notes repeated throughout the composition.

**Play the pairs of eighth notes a bit unevenly, long-short.

***The bass notes should fit with the first and third notes of the RH triplet.

NOTE: You may now begin to learn the first movement of Beethoven's famous *Moonlight Sonata,* if you wish. It is found in the "AMBITIOUS" section of this book, on pages 138–141.

The Primary Chords in C♯ Minor

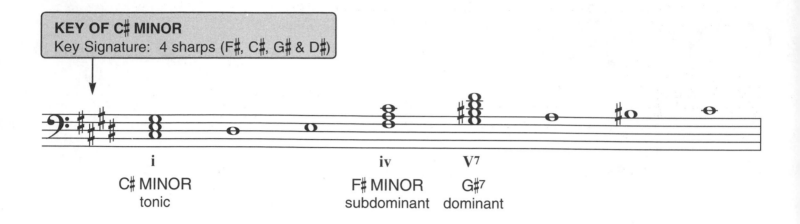

KEY OF C♯ MINOR
Key Signature: 4 sharps (F♯, C♯, G♯ & D♯)

i   iv   V⁷

C♯ MINOR   F♯ MINOR   G♯⁷
tonic   subdominant   dominant

The following positions are often used for smooth progressions:

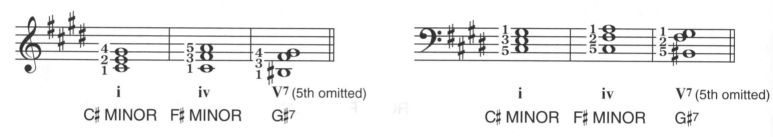

i   iv   V⁷ (5th omitted)   i   iv   V⁷ (5th omitted)

C♯ MINOR   F♯ MINOR   G♯⁷   C♯ MINOR   F♯ MINOR   G♯⁷

1. Add the C♯ MINOR key signature to each staff below.
2. Write the PRIMARY CHORDS in the key of C♯ MINOR, using the above positions.

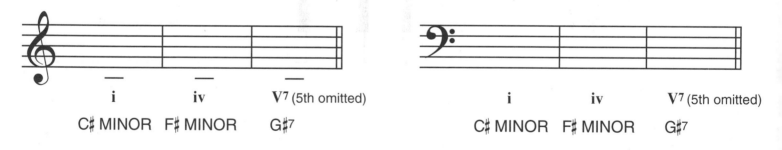

i   iv   V⁷ (5th omitted)   i   iv   V⁷ (5th omitted)

C♯ MINOR   F♯ MINOR   G♯⁷   C♯ MINOR   F♯ MINOR   G♯⁷

3. Write the ROMAN NUMERALS (i, iv, V⁷) in the boxes below.
4. Play.

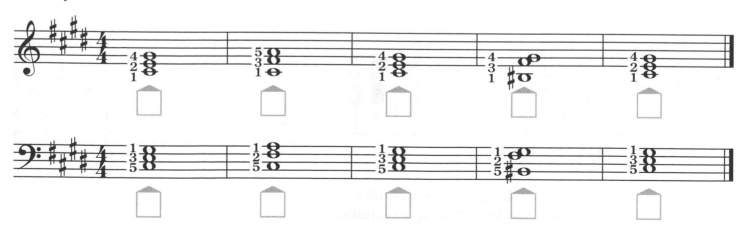

The Primary Chords in C♯ Minor—All Positions

1. In the blank measures after each ROOT POSITION chord, write the two INVERSIONS of the chord.

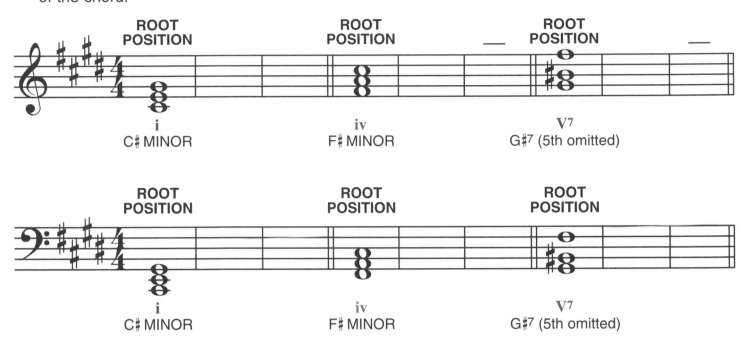

2. On the two keyboards to the right of each ROOT POSITION chord, write the letter names showing the two inversions of the chord.

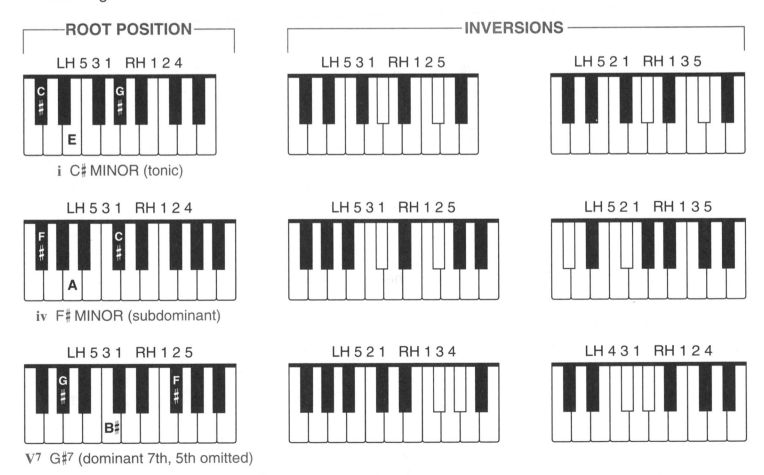

3. Play each chord shown on the above keyboards in any convenient place on your piano, first with LH, then with RH. Use the fingering shown above each keyboard.

JUST FOR FUN

Extend the fingers of LH & RH, palms downward, to tap the rhythms indicated with x's on the wood *above* the fall-board. Or if you prefer, drum on your thighs. Only the following rhythms are used:

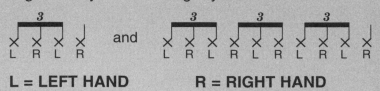

L = LEFT HAND   **R = RIGHT HAND**

THE TAP-DANCER

Molto moderato (*not* fast!)
light and detached

Willard A. Palmer

D. S. 𝄋 al 𝄉, then CODA

𝄉 CODA

The E♭ Major Scale

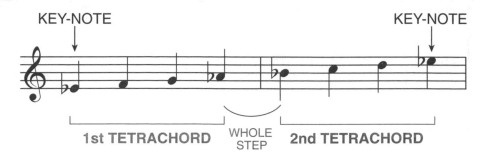

1st TETRACHORD WHOLE STEP **2nd TETRACHORD**

> **KEY OF E♭ MAJOR**
> Key Signature: 3 flats (B♭, E♭ & A♭)

After beginning with RH 3, the scale is fingered in groups of 1 2 3 4 – 1 2 3. End on 3.

After beginning with LH 3, the scale is fingered in groups of 3 2 1 – 4 3 2 1. End on 3.

THE E♭ MAJOR SCALE IN CONTRARY MOTION

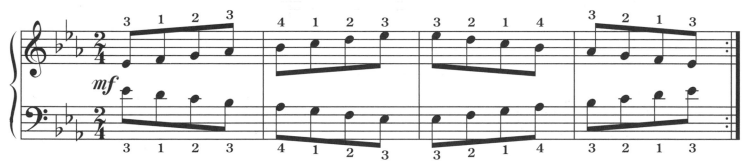

Practice this scale in parallel motion by playing the top two lines of this page with hands together.

SOLDIER'S JOY (HORNPIPE)

Traditional

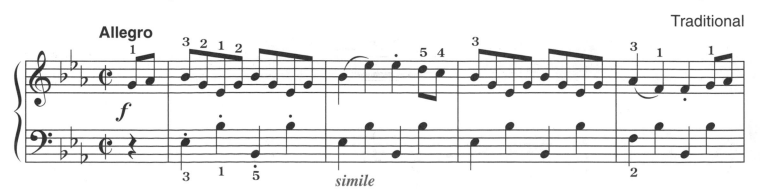

Fine

D. C. al Fine

Writing the E♭ Major Scale

1. Write the letter names of the notes of the E♭ MAJOR SCALE, from *left* to *right,* on the keyboard below. Be sure the WHOLE STEPS & HALF STEPS are correct!

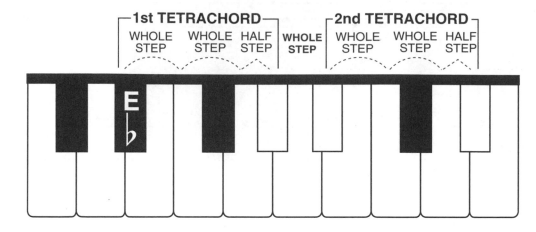

2. Check to be sure that you named the notes in the order of the musical alphabet. If you did, all the black keys will be named as *flats,* not *sharps.*

3. Complete the tetrachord beginning on E♭.
   Write one note over each finger number.

4. Complete the tetrachord beginning on B♭.
   Write one note over each finger number.

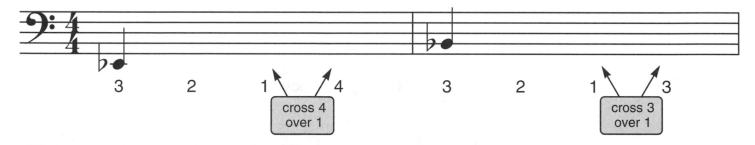

> **IMPORTANT!** *Only 4 fingers* are used to play the E♭ major scale with the LH and RH!
> The 5th finger is not used.

Beginning with LH 3, the scale is fingered in groups of 3 2 1 – 4 3 2 1; end on 3.

5. Write the fingering UNDER each note of the following LH scale.
6. Play with LH.

After beginning with RH 3, the finger groups then fall 1 2 3 4 – 1 2 3.

7. Write the fingering OVER each note of the following RH scale.
8. Play with RH.

The Primary Chords in E♭ Major

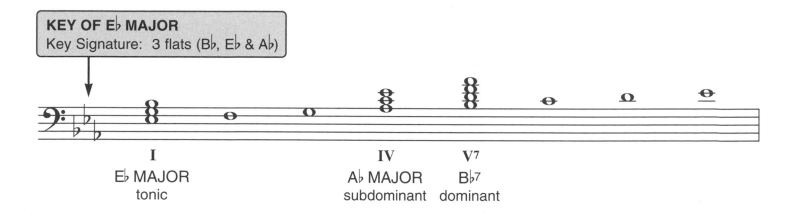

KEY OF E♭ MAJOR
Key Signature: 3 flats (B♭, E♭ & A♭)

I
E♭ MAJOR
tonic

IV
A♭ MAJOR
subdominant

V⁷
B♭⁷
dominant

The following positions are often used for smooth progressions:

I
E♭ MAJOR

IV
A♭ MAJOR

V⁷ (5th omitted)
B♭⁷

I
E♭ MAJOR

IV
A♭ MAJOR

V⁷ (5th omitted)
B♭⁷

1. Add the E♭ MAJOR key signature to each staff below.
2. Write the PRIMARY CHORDS in E♭ MAJOR, using the above positions.

I
E♭ MAJOR

IV
A♭ MAJOR

V⁷ (5th omitted)
B♭⁷

I
E♭ MAJOR

IV
A♭ MAJOR

V⁷ (5th omitted)
B♭⁷

3. Write the ROMAN NUMERALS (I, IV, V⁷) in the boxes below.
4. Play.

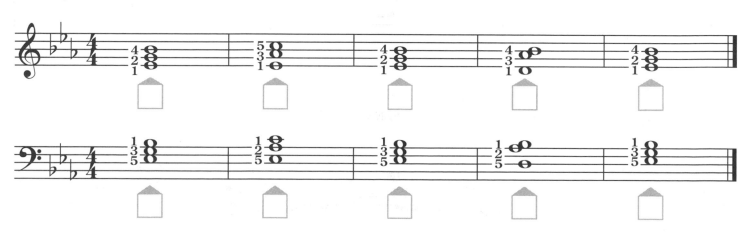

TOREADOR SONG from "Carmen"

George Bizet

*REMINDER: The three notes of a sixteenth-note triplet are played *evenly,* in the time of one EIGHTH NOTE.

ROCK-A MY SOUL

Spiritual

Allegro moderato
rhythmically

The Primary Chords in E♭ Major—All Positions

1. In the blank measures after each ROOT POSITION chord, write the two INVERSIONS of the chord.

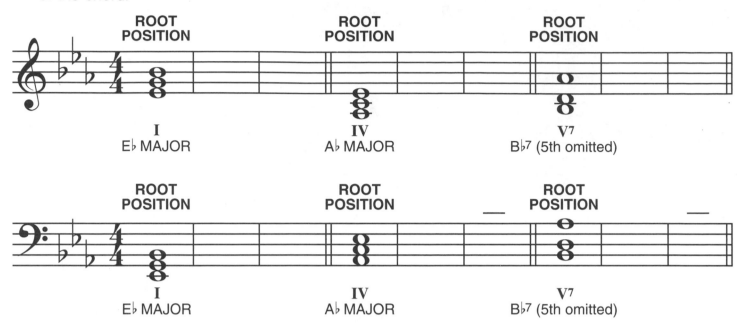

2. On the two keyboards to the right of each ROOT POSITION chord, write the letter names showing the two inversions of the chord.

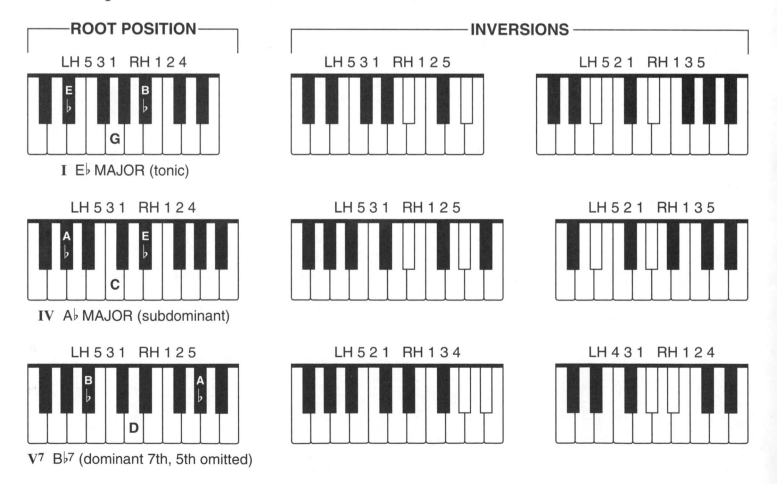

3. Play each chord shown on the above keyboards in any convenient place on your piano, first with LH, then with RH. Use the fingering shown above each keyboard.

Prelude in E♭ Major

Stephen Heller was born in Hungary but lived for many years in Paris. He played very successful concerts in Hungary, Poland, France and Germany. He was a friend of Schubert, Beethoven, Chopin, Liszt, and many of the other famous artists of his day. His compositions for piano were much in demand, with more than 160 volumes published.

Stephen Heller
(1813–1888)

The Key of C Minor (Relative of E♭ Major)

C MINOR is the relative of E♭ MAJOR.

Both keys have the same key signature (3 flats, B♭, E♭ & A♭).

THE C HARMONIC MINOR SCALE

Play with RH.

Play with LH.

THE C HARMONIC MINOR SCALE IN CONTRARY MOTION

Practice this scale in parallel motion by playing the top two lines of this page with hands together.

The NATURAL & MELODIC MINOR scales may also be practiced in parallel and contrary motion. The fingering is the same.

The NATURAL MINOR scale uses only the flats in the key signature (no B♮).

The MELODIC MINOR scale uses A♮ and B♮ ascending.
It descends like the natural minor.

VARIATIONS ON A SEA CHANTY

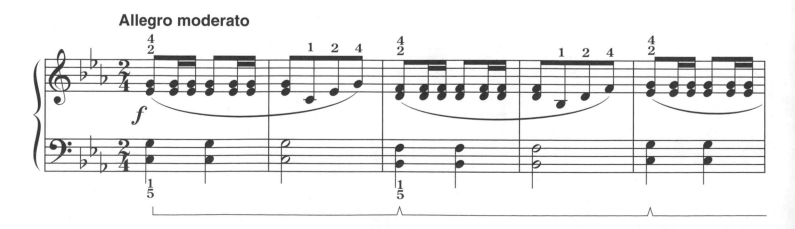

Scales in C Minor

REMEMBER: The RELATIVE MINOR begins on the 6th tone of the MAJOR SCALE.

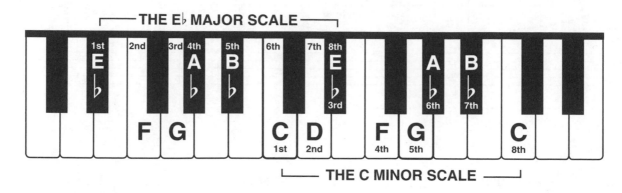

THE NATURAL MINOR SCALE: This scale uses *only* the tones of the relative major scale.

1. Play with hands separate, then together.

THE HARMONIC MINOR SCALE: The 7th tone (B♭) is raised 1 half step (to B♮), ascending & descending.

2. Add accidentals needed to change these NATURAL minor scales into HARMONIC minor scales.
3. Play with hands separate, then together.

THE MELODIC MINOR SCALE: 6th (A♭) and 7th (B♭) raised 1 half step (to A♮ & B♮) ASCENDING; DESCENDS like natural minor.

4. Add accidentals needed to change these NATURAL minor scales into MELODIC minor scales.
5. Play with hands separate.   6. (OPTIONAL) Play with hands together.

The Primary Chords in C Minor

KEY OF C MINOR
Key Signature: 3 flats (B♭, E♭ & A♭)

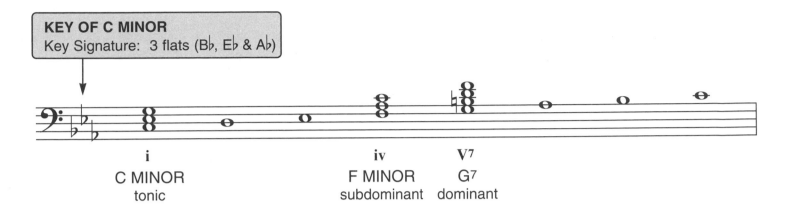

i		iv	V⁷
C MINOR		F MINOR	G⁷
tonic		subdominant	dominant

The following positions are often used for smooth progressions:

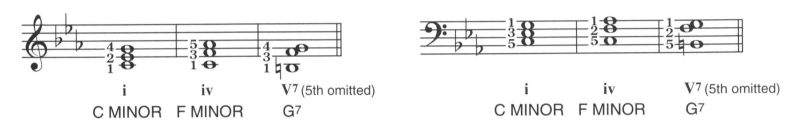

i	iv	V⁷ (5th omitted)		i	iv	V⁷ (5th omitted)
C MINOR	F MINOR	G⁷		C MINOR	F MINOR	G⁷

1. Add the C MINOR key signature to each staff below.
2. Write the PRIMARY CHORDS in the key of C MINOR, using the above positions.

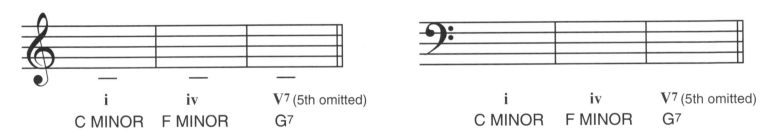

i	iv	V⁷ (5th omitted)		i	iv	V⁷ (5th omitted)
C MINOR	F MINOR	G⁷		C MINOR	F MINOR	G⁷

3. Write the ROMAN NUMERALS (**i**, **iv**, **V⁷**) in the boxes below.
4. Play.

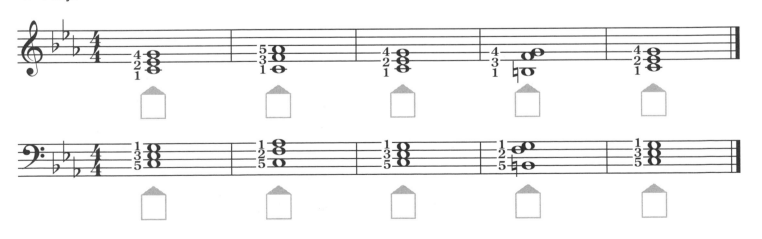

Prelude in C Minor

Alexander Morovsky

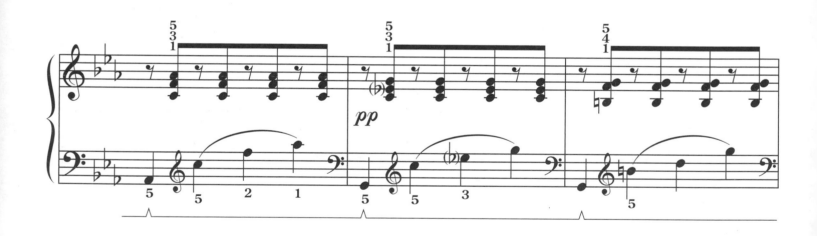

The Primary Chords in C Minor—All Positions

1. In the blank measures after each ROOT POSITION chord, write the two INVERSIONS of the chord.

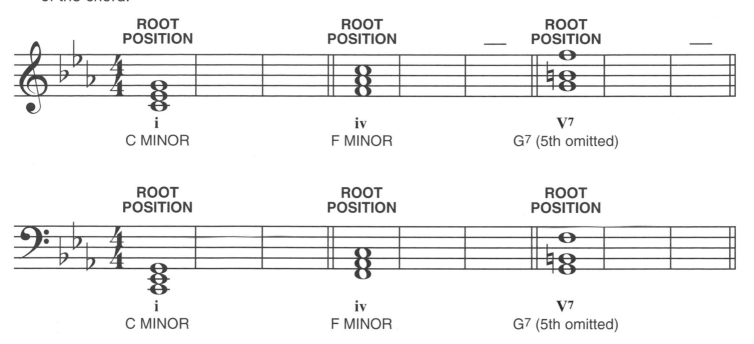

2. On the two keyboards to the right of each ROOT POSITION chord, write the letter names showing the two inversions of the chord.

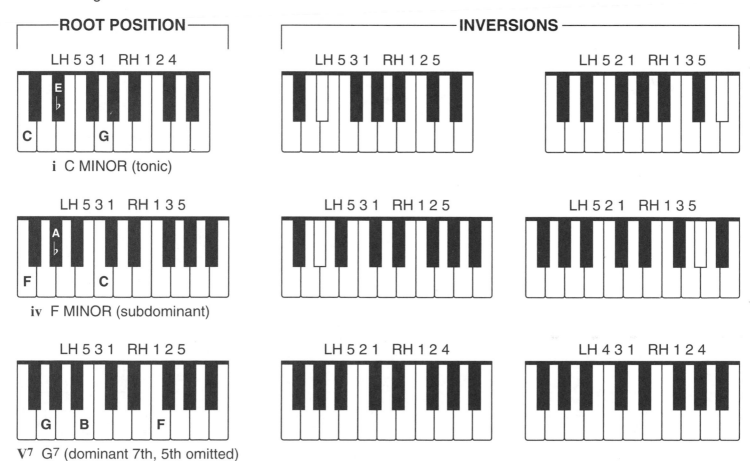

3. Play each chord shown on the above keyboards in any convenient place on your piano, first with LH, then with RH. Use the fingering shown above each keyboard.

The A♭ Major Scale

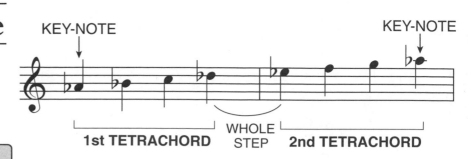

KEY-NOTE

KEY-NOTE

1st TETRACHORD | WHOLE STEP | 2nd TETRACHORD

KEY OF A♭ MAJOR
Key Signature: 4 flats (B♭, E♭, A♭ & D♭)

Play with RH.

Play with LH.

THE A♭ MAJOR SCALE IN CONTRARY MOTION

Practice this scale in parallel motion by playing the top two lines of this page with hands together.

DRY BONES

This piece will take you through the following major triads in all positions: A♭ major, A major, B♭ major, B major and C major. By using the suggestions at the bottom of the next page, you can use it to practice ALL the major triads!

Traditional

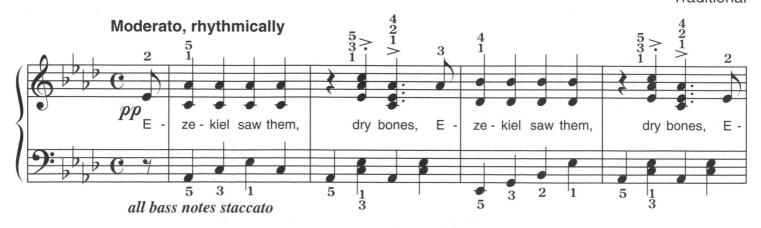

Moderato, rhythmically

pp

E - ze - kiel saw them,   dry bones,   E - ze - kiel saw them,   dry bones,   E -

all bass notes staccato

ze - kiel saw them, dry bones, Now hear the word of the Lord! A-well, the

head bone's con - nect-ed to the neck bone, The neck bone's con-nect-ed to the

back - bone, The back - bone's con - nect-ed to the hip bone, The

hip bone's con-nect-ed to the leg bone, The leg bone's con-nect-ed to the

foot bone, Now hear the word of the Lord! E -

*Play the eighth notes in long-short pairs.

**To play ALL major triads in all positions, continue moving one half step up the keyboard every two measures until the 5th finger of the LH plays G. Use the following sequence of bones:

head, neck, shoulder, back, hip, thigh, knee, shin, leg, heel, foot, toe.

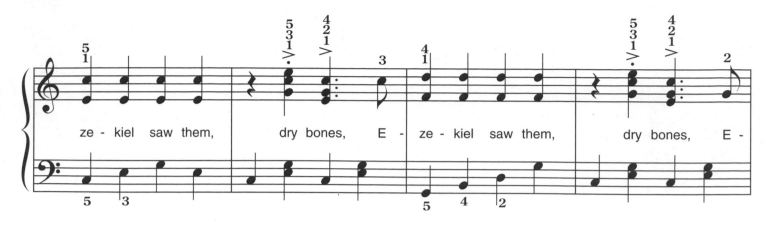

ze - kiel saw them, dry bones, E - ze - kiel saw them, dry bones, E -

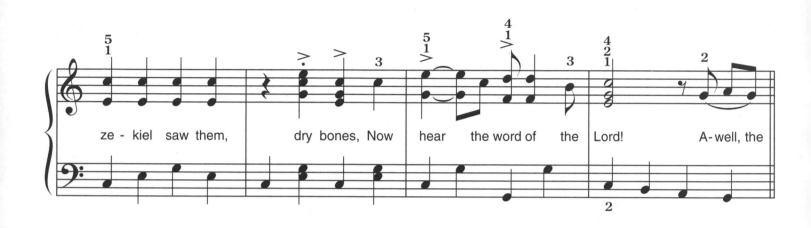

ze - kiel saw them, dry bones, Now hear the word of the Lord! A-well, the

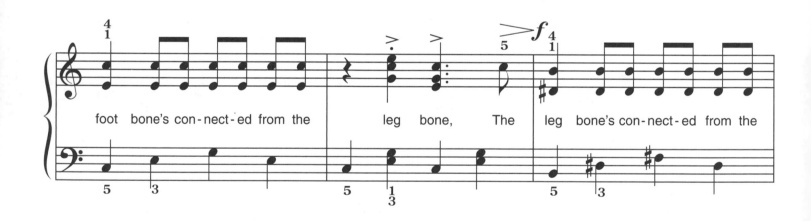

foot bone's con - nect - ed from the leg bone, The leg bone's con - nect - ed from the

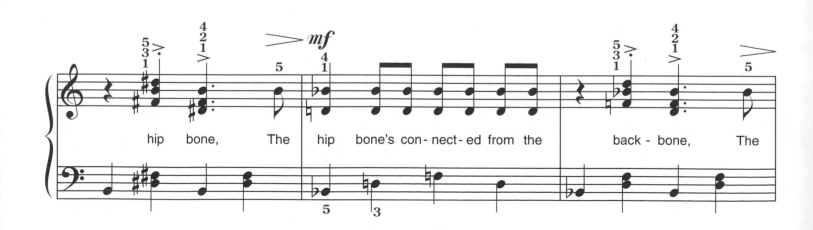

hip bone, The hip bone's con - nect - ed from the back - bone, The

Writing the A♭ Major Scale

1. Write the letter names of the notes of the A♭ MAJOR SCALE, from *left* to *right*, on the keyboard below. Be sure the WHOLE STEPS & HALF STEPS are correct!

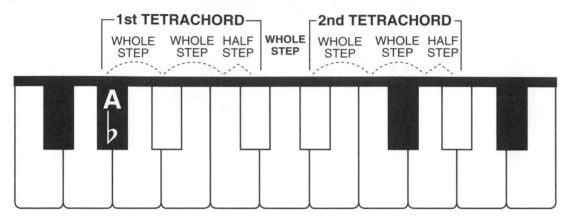

2. Check to be sure that you named the notes in the order of the musical alphabet. If you did, all the black keys will be named as *flats,* not *sharps!*

3. Complete the tetrachord beginning on A♭. Write one note over each finger number.

4. Complete the tetrachord beginning on E♭. Write one note over each finger number.

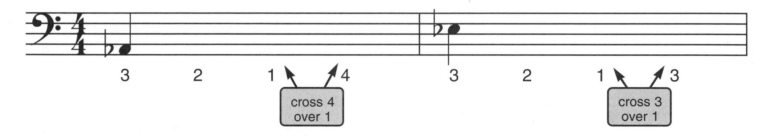

> **IMPORTANT!** *Only 4 fingers* are used to play the A♭ major scale with the LH! The 5th finger is not used.

Beginning with LH 3, the scale is fingered in groups of 3 2 1 – 4 3 2 1; end on 3.

5. Write the fingering UNDER each note of the following LH scale.
6. Play with LH.

After beginning with RH 3, the finger groups then fall 4 1 2 3 – 1 2 3.

7. Write the fingering OVER each note of the following RH scale.
8. Play with RH.

The Primary Chords in A♭ Major

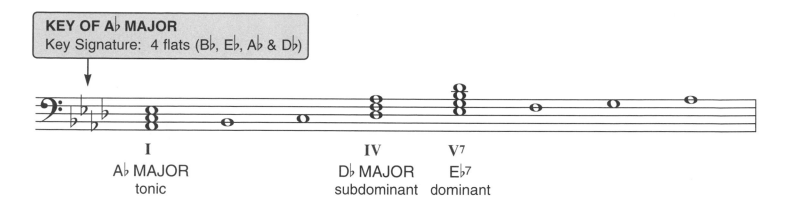

KEY OF A♭ MAJOR
Key Signature: 4 flats (B♭, E♭, A♭ & D♭)

I
A♭ MAJOR
tonic

IV
D♭ MAJOR
subdominant

V⁷
E♭⁷
dominant

The following positions are often used for smooth progressions:

I   IV   V⁷ (5th omitted)
A♭ MAJOR   D♭ MAJOR   E♭⁷

I   IV   V⁷ (5th omitted)
A♭ MAJOR   D♭ MAJOR   E♭⁷

1. Add the A♭ MAJOR key signature to each staff below.
2. Write the PRIMARY CHORDS in A♭ MAJOR, using the above positions.

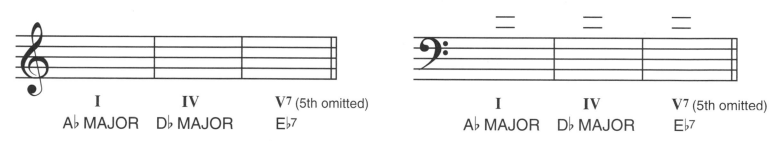

I   IV   V⁷ (5th omitted)
A♭ MAJOR   D♭ MAJOR   E♭⁷

I   IV   V⁷ (5th omitted)
A♭ MAJOR   D♭ MAJOR   E♭⁷

3. Write the ROMAN NUMERALS (**I, IV, V⁷**) in the boxes below.
4. Play.

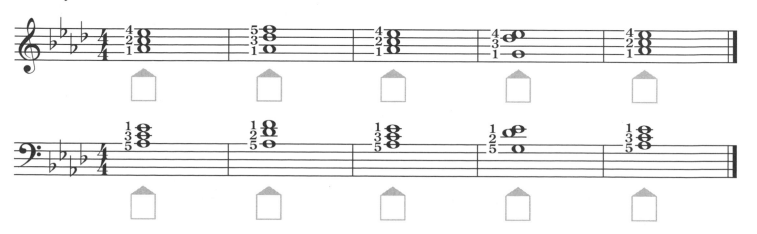

COUNTRY SONG

Willard A. Palmer

*Play the small note on the beat, together with the top note of the 3rd, then move rather quickly
  to the lower note of the 3rd. This produces a characteristic "country sound."

**Play the pairs of eighth notes long-short.

*REMINDER: *loco* means play as written (not *8va*).

The Primary Chords in A♭ Major—All Positions

1. In the blank measures after each ROOT POSITION chord, write the two INVERSIONS of the chord.

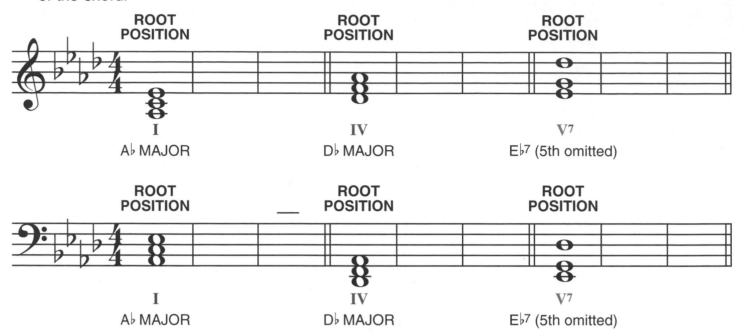

2. On the two keyboards to the right of each ROOT POSITION chord, write the letter names showing the two inversions of the chord.

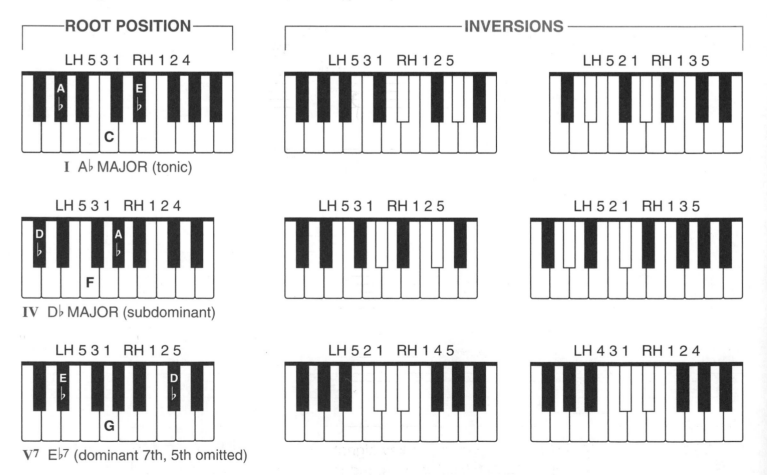

3. Play each chord shown on the above keyboards in any convenient place on your piano, first with LH, then with RH. Use the fingering shown above each keyboard.

Completing the Circle of 5ths (flats)

THE FLAT KEY SIGNATURES

Beginning with C and moving downward in 5ths counterclockwise, the order of keys around the circle is

C F B♭ E♭ A♭ D♭ G♭ C♭

Each key has one more flat than the previous one, as you move around the circle counterclockwise.

The key of C MAJOR has no flats.

The key of F MAJOR has 1 flat (B♭).

The key of B♭ MAJOR has 2 flats (B♭ & E♭), *etc.,* continuing around the circle until all the notes are flat.

The key of C♭ MAJOR has 7 flats: (B♭, E♭, A♭, D♭, G♭, C♭ & F♭).

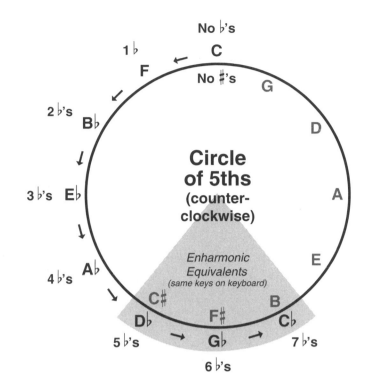

Copy the flats of each key signature in the blank measure following it.

F MAJOR
1♭ (B♭)

B♭ MAJOR
2♭'s (B♭, E♭)

E♭ MAJOR
3♭'s (B♭, E♭, A♭)

A♭ MAJOR
4♭'s (B♭, E♭, A♭, D♭)

D♭ MAJOR
5♭'s (B♭, E♭, A♭, D♭, G♭)

G♭ MAJOR
6♭'s (B♭, E♭, A♭, D♭, G♭, C♭)

C♭ MAJOR
7♭'s (B♭, E♭, A♭, D♭, G♭, C♭, F♭)

IMPORTANT! Notice that the flats in the key signatures occur in the order of the letters (moving counterclockwise) around the Circle of 5ths, beginning with B♭.

B♭ E♭ A♭ D♭ G♭ C♭ F♭

116

Reviewing: Ornaments

Ornaments are decorative notes added to melodies to make them more interesting and expressive.

Among the most important ornaments are:
- the LONG APPOGGIATURA
- the SHORT APPOGGIATURA
- the MORDENT
- the TRILL

THE LONG APPOGGIATURA Usually written as a small eighth note: ♪

The small note is played ON THE BEAT of the following large note, and borrows its time from the large note.

- If the large note is a whole, half or quarter note, the small note gets HALF its value.
- If the large note is a dotted note, the small note gets TWO-THIRDS of its value.

MATCHING PUZZLE

Draw lines connecting the dots on the matching boxes.

Written:

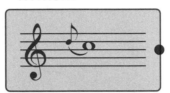

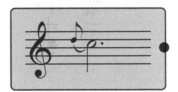

Played:

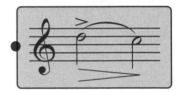

Score 20 for each pair.
Perfect score = 100.

YOUR SCORE: _____

THE SHORT APPOGGIATURA Written as a small eighth note with a cross-stroke: ♪

It is played VERY QUICKLY, almost together with the following large note.

Write an **S** in the box below each SHORT appoggiatura; an **L** below each LONG appoggiatura.

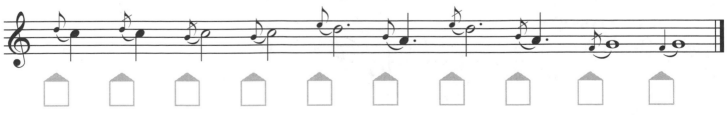

Score 10 for each correct answer.   Perfect score = 100. **YOUR SCORE:** _____

THE MORDENT ᨆ

Rapidly play: written note, note below written note, then written note again.

may be played: or   or

WALTZ WITH MORDENTS

1. In the measure above each mordent sign, write out the mordent in full, using one of the rhythms shown above. Be sure the first note is the same as the note that appears under the sign.
2. Play.

*For the lower tone of this mordent, use the raised 7th tone of the B minor scale (A♯).

Reviewing: Ornaments (continued)

THE TRILL

The TRILL is a rapid alternation of the written note with the note above it.
In some pieces, the trill is written out in notes. In others, a TRILL SIGN is used.

The most commonly used signs for the trill are: *tr* and *tr* 〰〰〰

In music of the 17th and 18th centuries, and most music of the early 19th century, the trill begins on the note ABOVE the written note. In later music the trill begins on the WRITTEN note. In *Alfred's Adult All-in-One Course,* you will always be shown how each trill should be played.

   may be played:    or

Trills do not always need to have an *exact* number of notes. They may be played faster than the notes above right indicate, with additional alternations of the two notes, but they must fit into the time value of the note.	Trills starting on the *upper* note are expressive and brilliant. They are like rapidly repeated upper appoggiaturas, and have a similar effect on the melody.	Trills starting on the *written* note are simply decorative, since they do not affect the melody.

MOZART'S TRILL EXERCISE

This valuable exercise was handed down to us by one of Mozart's most famous pupils, J. N. Hummel. If you practice it daily, you will be able to trill with all combinations of fingers with either hand!

Practice the entire exercise slowly at first. Gradually increase speed.

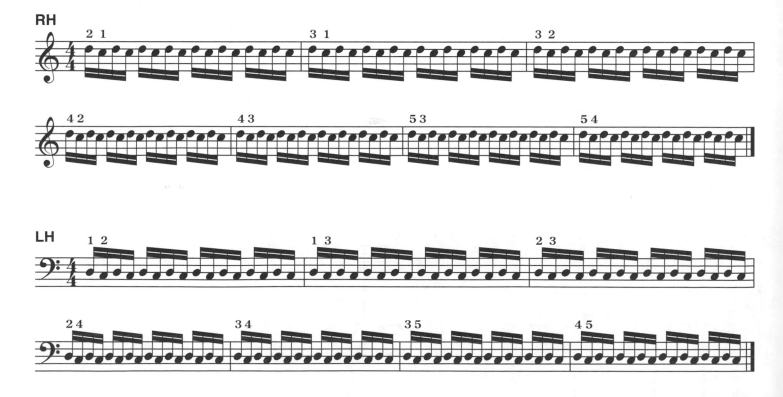

KING WILLIAM'S MARCH

This version of *KING WILLIAM'S MARCH,* one of Jeremiah Clarke's
most popular short pieces for keyboard, is taken from a manuscript,
dated 1704–07, in the British Library.

Jeremiah Clarke
(c. 1673–1707)

This piece is part of a larger composition for wind instruments, strings and drums. It is typical of the festive music played in the French courts in the early 1700s. It has become a familiar favorite because of its use as the theme for the popular television series, *Masterpiece Theatre.*

RONDEAU

Jean Joseph Mouret (1682–1753)
Transcribed by P. M. L.

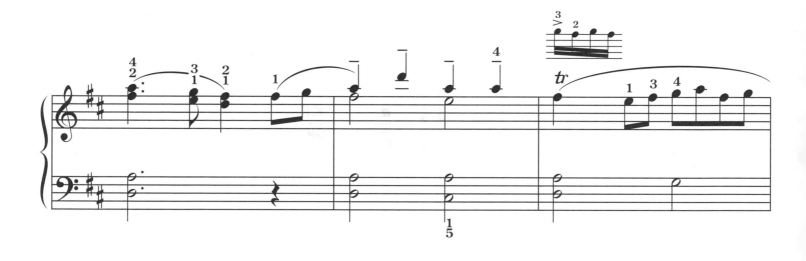

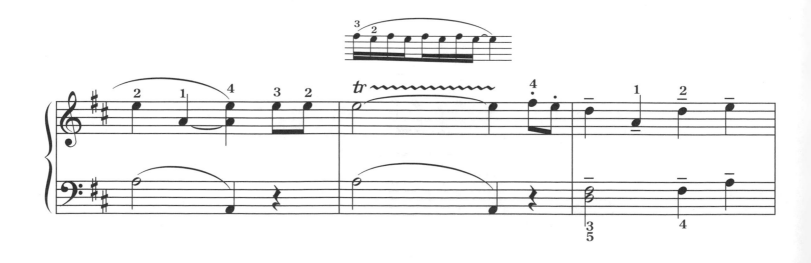

"AMBITIOUS" Section

This section (pages 122 through 141) is included for those who would like to play well-known classics in their original form, and who are ambitious enough to apply a little extra effort to do so.

Each one of these pieces is possible for anyone who has carefully studied all of the preceding material, and who is willing to put in a little careful and patient practice. The results should be very satisfying!

PRELUDE IN C MAJOR
from "The Well-Tempered Clavier," Vol. 1

Andante con moto*

Johann Sebastian Bach

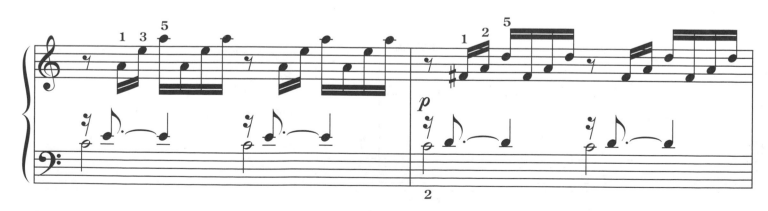

*****con moto** means "with motion." Avoid holding back or dragging the tempo.

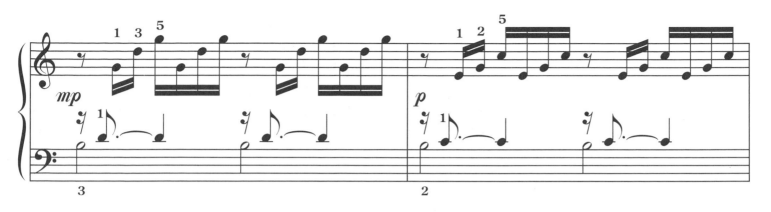

* Some editions have an extra measure added between this bar and the next. It is incorrect,
and is not to be found in any of J. S. Bach's manuscripts or those of his family members.

TRUMPET TUNE

This piece, played at many festive occasions and often used as a wedding march, is sometimes attributed to the great English composer, Henry Purcell. It was actually composed by one of his friends, Jeremiah Clarke (c. 1673–1707).

Alla marcia

Jeremiah Clarke

Thirty-Second Notes

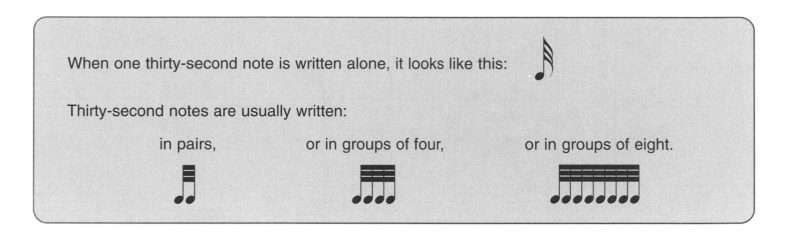

When one thirty-second note is written alone, it looks like this:

Thirty-second notes are usually written:

in pairs,   or in groups of four,   or in groups of eight.

Eight thirty-second notes are played
in the time of one quarter note.

There can be 32 thirty-second notes in one measure of COMMON ($\frac{4}{4}$) TIME!

Play several times—first ADAGIO, then ANDANTE, then ALLEGRO MODERATO.

Four thirty-second notes are played
in the time of one eighth note.

Play several times—first ADAGIO, then ANDANTE, then ALLEGRO MODERATO.

Toccata in D Minor

This piano transcription of the toccata from one of J. S. Bach's most famous organ works, *TOCCATA AND FUGUE IN D MINOR*, is not a simplification. All of the notes of the original are included.

Johann Sebastian Bach

*Pairs of eighths within the triplet pattern are played long-short to accommodate them to the basic triplet rhythm, according to the practice of the period. (This applies only to measures 6–14.)

Allegro moderato

Molto maestoso

Pesante means "heavy." Play each note with great firmness and emphasis.

Preparation for *FÜR ELISE* This piece, dedicated to a girl named *Elise* in 1810, is one of the most popular of all masterworks. The following measures contain unusual crossings of the LH 2nd finger over the thumb. Play the 3/4 measures first. Begin slowly, gradually increasing speed, then play the 3/8 measures.

FÜR ELISE

Ludwig van Beethoven

* *Moto* means "motion." *Poco moto* means "moving along a bit," or "rather fast."

**The pedal indications, derived from the original edition, have been adapted to the greater resonance of the modern piano and for modern "overlapping pedal" techniques.

***Most editions have D instead of E. The original edition and the only known fragmentary Beethoven manuscript both have E, as shown above.

* ⌣̇ The dots over or under the slurs indicate *portato*, sometimes called *mezzo staccato*.
The notes are only slightly separated (long but detached).

**Play the small notes very quickly, on the beat of the following large note.

* Note Beethoven's spelling of the diminished 7th chord: E G B♭ C♯. This means that it is an inversion
of the C♯dim7: C♯ E G B♭. The correct spelling of any diminished 7th in root position skips one letter
of the musical alphabet between each note.

135

* This chord is a G♯dim7 with the 3rd (B) omitted.

** In the original edition, the pedal is held from here to the end of the page. The resonance of the modern piano makes this impractical, in the opinion of the editors.

PRELUDE IN A MAJOR

Frédéric Chopin
Op. 28, No. 7

* This chord may be divided between the hands
  as follows. Play the small notes very quickly.
  (The composer did not indicate the wavy line.)

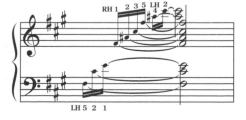

Sonata Quasi una Fantasia

"Moonlight Sonata" (First Movement)

When Beethoven's *SONATA QUASI UNA FANTASIA* (Sonata in the Style of a Fantasy) was first performed, a critic wrote that the first movement reminded him of "moonlight on Lake Lucerne." The public named it "Moonlight Sonata," and it is probably the most popular of Beethoven's piano works.

Ludwig van Beethoven
Op. 27, No. 2

Adagio sostenuto*

**Sostenuto* means "sustaining the tone."

Beethoven's instructions at the beginning of this piece are as follows:

> *This entire piece must be played very delicately and without dampers.*

The instruction "without dampers" was used on pieces written when the dampers were lifted by a knee lever rather than by a pedal. It means that the dampers should be off the strings. This is the same as our modern instructions to USE THE PEDAL. Thus "without dampers" = with pedal.

Modern pedal indications are added by the editors.

Dictionary of Musical Terms

Accelerando . . . . gradually increasing in speed

Accent sign (>) . . . . play with special emphasis

Adagio . . . . slow

Alla marcia . . . . in the style of a march, or "march-like"

Allargando . . . . becoming slower and broader

Allegretto . . . . rather fast; a little slower than *allegro*

Allegro . . . . quickly, happily, fast

Andante . . . . moving along (walking speed)

Animato . . . . animated; lively

Appoggiatura (♪ or ♪) . . a small ornamental note. Its purpose is to add expression to the melody.

Arpeggio . . . . a chord played in a "harp-like" fashion, broken or rolled

A tempo . . . . resume original speed

Atonal . . . . not in any definite key

Cantabile . . . . in a singing style

Coda . . . . an added ending

Coda sign (⊕) . . . . indication to proceed to *Coda,* which usually has the same sign

Common time (**C**) . . . . . . same as $\frac{4}{4}$ time

Con brio . . . . with vigor or brilliance

Con moto . . . . with motion (moving along)

Con spirito . . . . with spirit

Contrary motion . . . . hands moving in opposite directions

Crescendo (⟨) . . . . . gradually louder

Da Capo al Fine . . . . repeat from the beginning to the word "Fine"

Dal Segno al Fine . . . . . . repeat from the sign 𝄌 to the word "Fine"

Development . . . . the part of a composition in which the main themes (subjects) are treated with freedom and imagination

Diminuendo (⟩) . . . . gradually softer

Dolce . . . . sweetly

Double flat (♭♭) . . . . lowers a flatted note one *half* step, or a natural note one *whole* step

Double sharp (𝄪) . . . . raises a sharped note one *half* step, or a natural note one *whole* step

Elision . . . . when one slur ends just as another begins on the same note

Espressivo . . . . expressively

Exposition . . . . the first statement of the main theme or themes of a composition

Fermata (⌒) . . . . hold the note or notes under the sign longer

Fine . . . . the end

Forte (*f*) . . . . loud

Fortissimo (*ff*) . . . . very loud

Grandioso . . . . in a grand and majestic manner

Grazioso . . . . gracefully

Interval . . . . the distance from one note to the next

Largo . . . . very slow

Legato . . . . smoothly connected

Leggiero . . . . lightly

Loco . . . . as written (not *8va*)

Maestoso . . . . majestically

Meno mosso . . . . slower

Mezzo forte (*mf*) . . . . moderately loud

Mezzo piano (*mp*) . . . . . . moderately soft

Moderato . . . . a moderate speed

Molto . . . . much, very

Mordent (⌁) . . . . an ornament that alternates the written note with the tone below. It is played quickly: written note, lower note, written note.

Morendo . . . . dying away

Moto . . . . motion

Octave sign (*8va*) . . . . . . play 8 scale tones (one octave) higher when the sign is above the notes; 8 scale tones lower when the sign is below the notes

Parallel motion . . . . hands moving in the same direction

Pesante . . . . heavy

Pianissimo (*pp*) . . . . very soft

Piano (*p*) . . . . soft

Più . . . . more

Più *f* . . . . louder

Più mosso . . . . faster

Poco . . . . little, small

Poco a poco . . . . little by little

Poco moto . . . . moving along a bit; rather fast

Polytonal . . . . in two or more keys at the same time

Portato . . . . a manner of playing between legato & staccato, sometimes called *mezzo staccato.* The notes are only slightly separated (long but detached).

Prestissimo . . . . very fast

Presto . . . . fast

Recapitulation . . . . a repetition of the main theme or themes of a piece, after a development or other section has been heard

Repeat sign (▥) . . . . repeat from the beginning, or from ▤

Risoluto . . . . resolutely, boldly

Ritardando . . . . gradually slowing

Ritenuto . . . . literally "holding back." Slowing down the tempo immediately.

Scherzo . . . . a musical joke

Segue . . . . continue

Sequence . . . . repetition of a musical pattern, beginning on a higher or lower note

Sforzando (*sf*) . . . . forcing; sudden ly loud on one note or chord

Simile . . . . continue in the same manner

Sostenuto . . . . sustaining the tone

Staccato . . . . short, detached

Tempo . . . . rate of speed

Tenuto (–) . . . . hold for full value; emphasize slightly

Tetrachord . . . . 4 tones having a pattern of *whole step—whole step—half step*

Theme . . . . a complete musical idea or subject

Tonal . . . . in a definite key

Tranquillo . . . . calm; tranquil

Triad . . . . a three-note chord: root, 3rd, 5th

Trill (⌁ or *tr*) . . . . an ornament that alternates the written note with the next scale tone above, several or many times

Vivace . . . . lively; faster than *allegro,* but slower than *presto*

Certificate of Award

This is to certify that

_____

has successfully completed
Alfred's Adult All-in-One Course, Level 3.

Date _____

Teacher _____